Janice (Jan) Ballard

*Aloha!
Allison
Ballard
July 2011*

THE LONGEST JOURNEY

Two Women's Parallel Stories
of Grief and Healing

Outskirts Press, Inc.
Denver, Colorado

The Longest Journey
Two Women's Parallel Stories of Grief and Healing
All Rights Reserved.
Copyright © 2011 Janice (Jan) Holman Ballard and Allison (Cammie) Ballard
v2.0

Outskirts Press, Inc.
http://www.outskirtspress.com

ISBN: 978-1-4327-7381-6

Outskirts Press and the "OP" logo are trademarks belonging to Outskirts Press, Inc.

PRINTED IN THE UNITED STATES OF AMERICA

"Sometimes in your life you will go on a journey.
It will be the longest journey you have ever taken.
It is the journey to find yourself."

-Katherine Sharp

We dedicate this book to the memory of
Henry (Hank) Ballard, 1940-1999
and James Henry Bonfitto, 1948-2000

HIGH FLIGHT

Oh, I have slipped
the surly bonds of Earth,
and danced the skies
on laughter-silvered wings;
Sunward I've climbed
and joined the tumbling mirth
of sun-split clouds
and done a hundred things
you have not dreamed of...
and while with silent,
lifting mind I've trod
the high, untrespassed
sanctity of space,
put out my hand
and touched the face of God.

–Part of a poem by John Gillespie Magee, Jr.

Thank you to our focus group of readers for their time and efforts in improving this book. Thanks also to each of you who has walked this journey with us....you know who you are!

FAMILY RELATIONSHIPS

Henry Allison Ballard (Hank) and Janice Kaye Holman Ballard (Jan)
Daughters: Babs, Lita and Cammie
(Cammie is a family nickname; her given name is Allison)

Babs now lives in Washington state and is married to Buddy
Daughters Haley and Jessica, married to Gene

Lita lives in Florida and is married to Ken
Son Nicholas and daughters Sarah and Natali, married to Justin

Cammie (Allison) lives in Indiana
Son Jacob and daughter India
stepdaughters Amanda and Roma, married to Leslie

Carl, neighbor, friend and minister

PART 1

ALONG THE ROAD

I walked a mile with Pleasure;
She chattered all the way,
But left me none the wiser
For all she had to say.
I walked a mile with Sorrow
And ne'er a word said she;
But oh, the things I learned from her
When Sorrow walked with me.

– Robert Browning Hamilton

JAN
November 1999

Night fills the room. Dawn has not yet arrived, but Hank is gone. He died just before midnight. And I have been transported to a far away country with strange customs and foreign words. The land of widowhood. The word rolls around my tongue ugly, bleak and hard to pronounce. Widow. It does not seem descriptive of who I am or who I have been.

Waiting for streaks of early morning light, I pick up my notebook and pen. Over the past 18 months, I have kept careful records of Hank's medicines and treatments and doctor visits. I have been his advocate, making sure he received the medical care he needed. Now I am a widow.

This journey into the unfamiliar world of cancer began with Hank experiencing shortness of breath in the spring of 1998. Six weeks of tests, blood draws, X-Rays, CT scans, a collapsed lung, the testing of fluid drawn from his chest cavity and ultimately a lung biopsy finally told us what we didn't want to hear. He had mesothelioma–a cancer of the lining of the lung, usually caused by exposure to asbestos 30 to 40 years prior to symptoms. The prognosis wasn't good and treatment options were minimal. Most mesothelioma patients die within 18 months of the first symptoms.

The family was gathered in a small hospital consultation room when we finally received the diagnosis. Such a big truth for such a small room. Together we went to Hank, still recovering from the biopsy, and waited for his dreaded question, "What did they find?"

It was one of many pivotal moments. As we shared the diagnosis, I assured him we would look for the best doctors and the best treatment center. He reached for me, trying to come up out of the bed. I leaned down to him and we embraced and cried together.

"It's been a good run, hasn't it?" he asked.

"I'm so thankful we found each other when we were so young and have had 45 years together," I answered. "And I'm not ready for it to be over yet."

"Yes, I may go down, but I want to go down swinging," he resolved.

"We are facing some serious stuff Hank, and we are going to have to be real with each other. We have to give each other the freedom to cry or talk about whatever we're feeling and agree that we're not going to hide from each other." Determined to face this challenge together, we left the hospital and with the help of our three daughters researched and learned more than we ever dreamed about mesothelioma, our unwelcome, uninvited guest.

Our story ended in cancer, but it had a wonderful beginning:

I am 14 years old and it is my first day of high school. A new boy walks into my freshman science class. He has just moved to our little town in Western Kentucky and is so cute! I see him and something shifts. I don't know his name, but I know he is the one.

"Today I saw the boy I'm going to marry," I tell my best friend that afternoon, walking home from school. She laughs. "I'll bet you a dime I'll marry him," I say. "Let's put two dimes in an envelope. If I marry him, I get the dimes. If not, you get the dimes."

The dimes were eventually misplaced, but I won the bet. Hank and I married young and within six years we had three little girls, Babs, Lita and Cammie. It took Hank ten years to get through college, working full time and going to school part time, but life was good. He got a good job and promotions that took us to Ohio, Michigan and, finally, Indiana.

The girls grew up, married, had children and Hank and I continued enjoying life and one another. Then mesothelioma came calling. Everything changed as we fought for his life and our life together as we knew it. A Florida doctor offered hope, so we spent 10 months living in Tampa where he received treatment from the Moffit Cancer Center. Hank had a lung, part of his heart lining and part of his diaphragm removed, followed by months of chemotherapy and radiation. In June 1999, we returned to our Indiana home thinking we had beaten cancer. We had several good weeks before beginning the downward spiral that led to his death.

As he grew worse, our world shrunk. Though we were back home in Indiana, Hank couldn't climb the stairs to our bedroom. Furniture was moved out of the living room and replaced with a twin bed for him and another twin mattress on the floor for me. Then a hospital bed replaced the twin bed. Then a wheelchair and oxygen tank moved in. Slowly our world was reduced to three rooms. But even as our living space shrunk, our love grew.

From the beginning, we chose to talk openly and share our true feelings with one another. We hugged a lot and cried a lot. And that last summer we talked a lot about him leaving me. He was 59 and I was 58. We had been together 45 years, married 42 years. He said my part, learning to live without him, would be the hardest. So he taught me things I would need to know, things he had always done. Like how to trim the bushes, put filters in the furnace, take care of the finances. He told me how sorry he was that he would not be with me at my dying time.

In those months of illness, faced with his impending death, we grew even closer and more in love. Putting aside all the things that don't matter, we found the only thing left was our love and being together. I have no idea how I will survive without him.

As I practice saying the word widow, I begin the longest journey I will ever make-the journey to know myself and learn to live without being the wife of Hank Ballard. Our long love has developed deep roots. I hope they will help me as I walk life's road alone. I pick up my notebook and pen and begin to write.

CAMMIE
November 1999

I can hear the phone ringing inside, but don't jump to get it. I just keep scraping ice cream out of the bottom of my bowl. It's early November, unseasonably warm and I am sitting on my front porch. I stir the melted vanilla into the remaining chocolate syrup. Should I just let it all melt together, or should I stir it up? Oh, the choices we must make!

"Mom, the phone's ringing!" the kids yell out at me through the open door.

"I hear it," I answer. But I don't move towards it. I just keep spooning. I know who it is. Every cell in my body knows who it is. Mother is calling to tell me Daddy is dying. Not "deteriorating slowly over a period of time to his eventual final moment." He's dying. Tonight. She's calling to tell me we should start the 45-minute drive from our house to theirs.

For two years, I have jumped at every phone call, thrown dirty clothes into suitcases, flown back and forth to Florida, ripped the kids out of school on a moment's notice, renegotiated deadlines at work, rescheduled college tests, done whatever I could to be there as needed. For them, for me, for the kids. Now that it's come to this final good-bye, the only thing I'm moving is my spoon and slowly at that as I savor each sweet bite. But the ice cream is gone. The phone is ringing again. "I've got it," I sigh, grab the bowl and go inside.

I drive to my parents' house, pull up to the end of the cul-de-sac and park by the curb. The driveway is full of cars. Both my sisters and their families have already arrived from out of state. I stand at the edge of the yard, looking across the span of lawn that stretches between the house and me. Daddy's favorite music wafts out of the open windows. A slight breeze moves the curtains. Everything else is still. Bare trees frame the moment. I take a deep breath and my daughter, India's, hand. We walk together as my son, Jacob, runs ahead.

Inside, the house is calm. My sisters, their husbands and my nieces mill around, making quiet conversation. Daddy lies in the hospital bed in the front room. We all take turns moving in and out. Everyone except Jacob. My 13-year-old walks in and sits on the footstool that Mother placed beside Daddy's bed so they could see each other eye to eye. I watch my son take my dying father's hand. I go looking for a shot glass or a tumbler–I know Daddy has whiskey somewhere in this house.

"How are you doing?" I ask my brother-in-law, Buddy, as I open the bottle of Wild Turkey. Wild Turkey? Are you kidding me?

"We're doing all right," he says. I fill my glass and offer Bud the bottle, but he declines. On a better day, I would refuse Wild Turkey myself, but tonight I take it straight, on the rocks.

Whiskey in hand, I go back into the front room. Jacob hasn't moved. Mother is sitting at the foot of Daddy's bed. She and Jacob are talking to each other, but Jacob's eyes are glued to Daddy's unresponsive face. Mother is telling us that the nurse started morphine this afternoon. Other people come into the room. Casual conversation. Soft laughter. Quiet tears.

"Do you think he can hear us?" I ask.

"He can hear us," Jacob says certainly. "He's listening. He knows we're here."

Time passes. A sort of aimless wandering fills the house. My glass and I move with the flow of traffic, in and out and around…we are all midwives to his passage, waiting for him to move through.

Jacob's dark head leans in close to Daddy's ear. "It's okay for you to go," I hear him say quietly. "You don't have to stay here anymore. We're all okay. Thank you for everything. You've done a good job." I stir my ice with my finger just to hear the clink. When exactly during the last two years of illness and hospitals and holding on and letting go did my preteen son become so wise to the ways of death?

We all gather in the room as Dad's breath becomes more labored.

It struggles in. It struggles out. I feel a moment of panic as if I should do something, but yielding is all that is left to be done. His breath pauses and stops. He's gone. Or he's just arrived, depending on your point of view. Mother gives each family unit time alone with his body. My little family goes first because Jacob is still glued to his spot.

India buries her head in my belly. I run my fingers through her soft blonde curls. "Is there anything you want to say to Daddy Hank?" I ask her. She shakes her head no and peeks a look at his body. I look at Jacob. He shakes his head no as well. He leaves the stool and joins us at the foot of the bed. I have nothing to say either. I have spent every Wednesday afternoon with Daddy for the last few months, providing respite for mother. He and I have talked about many things. Everything I had to say, I said while he was alive. So the three of us simply sit, looking at his now-peaceful body as the stillness wraps around us. The music is still playing. The curtains still move in the breeze. But things have changed; nothing will ever be the same. We experience the shift together and leave the room.

JAN
November 1999

When I wake up the next morning, Hank is still dead. And so is the phone. So many calls to make, yet there is no dial tone. My head is as full as it is groggy so I make a list. So many details to take care of–how can there still be so many things needing attention, now that he is gone?

My son-in-law, Bud, drives me to a nearby town to share the news with my elderly father. Each passing mile is another moment that he is dead. We make phone calls from a pay phone. Each call is another moment of truth.

"Hank died last night. Yes, he died at home. Yes, he died peacefully. Yes, we were all together." I grow weary of these words–of saying them and hearing them. I am saying yes, but I am screaming no. Inside, I am screaming. I ask a friend to make the remaining calls and I go home.

The oxygen people come and remove the tank and tubing. The hospice people come and remove the hospital bed. They leave such emptiness in their wake. He's left such emptiness in his absence. The family helps me arrange the house. We try to put things in their place, some new post-Hank place. We try to bring order to this undercurrent of chaotic change.

Neighbors and friends drop by. Ken, another son-in-law, flies out. My sister, Jennifer, flies in from South Carolina. Hank's mother, brother and sister-in-law drive up from Kentucky. In the midst of all this coming and going I am suddenly, unexpectedly alone. For the first time in many days. For the first time in many months. For the first time in many years. This truth wraps around me like a mourning veil that disguises my identity as wife and partner. I am camouflaged–I don't even know who I am without that "Mrs." in front of my name. I have been with him most of my life.

I prayed I would be with him in death. I prayed that when it was time, he would go quickly, gently into the night without pain. All these gifts were granted and I am grateful. I am also grateful he had me make funeral arrangements before he died. At the time, I didn't want to think my way through the business of his death, but no matter how hard it was to do then, it would have been much harder to do now. My head swims with details of calling hours and a funeral here in Indiana. Then more calling hours and a graveside service in our hometown in Western Kentucky have to be arranged. And I need to rent a van—friends Diane and John are driving his body home in a van.

Then I'll take another trip to my granddaughter's wedding later this month in Ohio. Hank wanted to be there so badly he was willing to go in his sweat pants and the tuxedo T-shirt Babs bought him to wear with them. And Thanksgiving is just around the corner. We were looking forward to sharing one last holiday season together. How can there still be so much life now that he is dead? My daughter, Lita, says she and granddaughters Natali and Sarah will stay with me until the weekend after Thanksgiving. And for that I am also grateful. For once they leave, I will truly be alone, trying to find my place, a new sense of order, in all this emptiness. Can I do this? I am tired and achy and need a nap.

My thoughts wander to years before: I can see my father standing on his porch, waving goodbye to Hank and me as we drive off after my mother's funeral. I am sobbing in both this memory and this moment. My Daddy was 59 when Mother died suddenly at 58. Now at age 59 I still feel way too young to grow up and I know that at age 59 Hank was way too young to die.

"We weren't finished yet!" I cry to no one. "We still had things to do, important things!" We had planned on spending years together sitting on our screened porch, watching the birds in the woods in our back yard, working cross word puzzles, playing dominoes, walking through the woods. We had planned to walk hand in hand into the sunset of our lives...I don't want to be like my parents. I don't want to be a widow. And I don't want to be alone. All I want is Hank. The sobbing turns into a numbing calm that helps me do what needs to be done.

The phone has apparently been resurrected. It rings again and again. We are bombarded with calls that my girls help me answer; we surf each one as if it is a wave. The day becomes a precarious balancing act as we strive to be neither immersed nor detached. Then comes the tsunami—I read a letter from Hank that he asked me to save until after he died. We are no longer surfing, we are not even floating; we are drowning in our tears.

HANK

(written 7-22-98)

Dearest Jan,

    If you are reading this, I have died. There are some things I want to leave with you. Number one and foremost is that I love you very much and have loved you for 44 years. We had a good life for which I am thankful.

    Looking back, there are very few things I would change. At the time there were things that seemed intolerable, but now I realize they were only character builders. Together, we built a life, raised a family, and prepared for retirement. We did a pretty good job: our girls are solid women able to take care of themselves; we have good friends and we have the means to do what we want to do. All of this was possible because we did it as a team. You did what you were good at and I did what I was good at. As far as retirement is concerned, we had three good years before I got sick which is more than a lot of people have. When I hear people say they would drive each other crazy in retirement, I am thankful for you and your loving, sweet personality. You have made our life together great.

    In today's world, 58 years is young, but it was a good and full 58 years. Think of it: in our peer group we were the first to marry, the first to have children and the first to retire. We have crammed a lot of living into my 58 years, much more than others get in 80 or 90 years. Not only did we have quantity, we also had quality life. Each stage we went through was a new experience that we handled and that proved to be a learning experience. We did many things we didn't think we could do. And we did them well: we moved to new locations, met new people, created a new life, succeeded with new jobs and dealt with all the different stages of our girls' lives.

Now we move into yet another stage of life. Yes, death is but another stage of life. We will successfully deal with this stage as we have dealt with all the others. Only this time my part will be easy while you must work at your part. Make a new life for yourself as you have done so many times in the past. You now know how so go ahead and do it. Find happiness to finish out your term on this earth. May it be a long, happy and rewarding period. After, and only after a long successful journey, will I meet you at the eastern gate of heaven.

As always,
Lots of love,
Hank

PS Kiss the girls and grandkids for me

JAN
November 1999

I look for his obituary in the paper. How strange to see his life portrayed as a paragraph collection of facts. These vitals are as limiting as his body became. They don't describe what a treasure he was. They don't explain how special he was. I am thankful to have known him. I am thankful that I shared his life.

Today is his calling; it is time to go. I am not numb. I am fully intact, in touch with my body and my feelings. And the starkness of everything. My senses brim with senseless detail as if I am playing a game of Memory and will be quizzed at the end of the day. The wool of my coat brushes against my legs. The smooth glass of the car window cools my hands and forehead. I look out at a beautiful day with bare November trees silhouetted against a sunny blue sky.

"I believe I can fly." At the funeral home, Hank's theme song fills the room as I stand alone at his casket. He is dressed in his blue and white University of Kentucky non-jogging suit. His T-shirt says, "Don't give up, don't ever give up." He never did. "I'm not afraid," he told the chaplain who came to visit him in the hospital. "I'm still not convinced I can't fly." That is how he lived his life. That is how he met his death.

The room is full of his music and family photographs and memorabilia. Front and center is the pink "Still Not Convinced You Can't Fly" poster Babs made for Hank when he was in the hospital; it has all our handprints and names on it. I move around these displayed fragments, surrounded by the trivia from our lives. I am reminded of the de-coupaged collages I used to make, cutting tiny pictures out of magazines and gluing them and other small items onto stained pieces of wood. They were titled, "This is my Life." Yes, this is my life I remind myself, though it seems this stained board must have been made for someone else.

People stream steadily through with hugs and comforting words, people who knew him, who knew us. I am surrounded by family and friends, real flesh-and-bone, air-breathing people, but I am carried by angels. I imagine Hank's new spiritual body exploring his new environment. It has been three days. I sleep. I eat. I cry. My faith is strong.

This strength carries me through a beautiful funeral service. I am so calm. I am calm while people pray and while friends speak. I am calm while Cammie sings "Amazing Grace." I am amazed at how calm I am. I wonder if I am really okay; I have entered a surreal world of uncertainty where things may not be what they seem.

Do I really hear normal conversation? Is someone actually laughing? Our emotions bounce around like ping pong balls that have no set pathways. Suddenly, Lita bursts into tears. "I'm ready for him not to be dead anymore!" she cries.

"Me too," I sigh. "Me too."

Hank's brother, Bob, pulls me aside. "I don't know how to live without my big brother in my life," he cries. "Hank always helped me when we were growing up. He always went ahead of me when we had to pick cotton and strawberries. He would go first so he could pick the hard ones; he'd leave the easy ones for me." I don't know how to live without him either, but we'll both learn.

Later in the day, back at home, my stress grows into a sinus infection and I no longer feel well. We are all worn out as we pack for the trip to Kentucky. We leave tomorrow. Eight hours in a van with two kids, two teens and Daddy who is elderly and does not travel well. I dread the trip, but am grateful for family. It is after midnight when everyone gathers in the living room. My mattress on the floor becomes an oasis where we eat popcorn and talk. We are our own lullaby, soothing each other through the unknown.

"Oh, Hank." I say it over and over as I did so many times during the last weeks of his life. It is days after his death and I am in a hotel room in Kentucky, worn out and bone tired. I ache all over; even my eyes hurt, but we survived the trip. We made it. Tomorrow will be visitation at another funeral home and the last time we will see Hank's earthly body before the graveside service. How I have loved that body and the spirit that it housed.

"Oh, Hank." I say it over and over.

CAMMIE
Memory 1998

Mother calls and says Daddy still isn't feeling better. I haven't been paying close enough attention to track the details, but I know it's now been several months and several rounds of antibiotics. I have a nagging concern that something more serious may be going on...he's been smoking cigarettes for such a long time.

I get on the internet and do some research. I read about small cell and non-small cell lung cancers. I learn that cancer settles in bronchial tubes, in air sacs, in glands, near the surface, or not. It is diagnosed by stages and symptoms include shortness of breath, wheezing and coughing among others. This doesn't feel good, doesn't feel good at all. Fortunately, we don't have to worry about mesothelioma. A rare aggressive cancer with no association to smoking; it is almost always caused by exposure to asbestos.

I silently wait for a biopsy. I certainly see one coming. But of course, it must unfold in its own good time. Mom hasn't mentioned one yet. So I work, I go to school, I parent, I dance, I drum, I write. I am the Development Director of a small non-profit modern dance organization in Northeast Indiana. I write grants seeking funds to fulfill the agency's mission to develop human potential through movement and dance. I like to point out our mission is not to create dancers. Although that is a nice byproduct, our mission is to encourage human beings to grow into greater wholeness. We use dance and movement and rhythm to provide a framework that guides and contains that process.

I see myself as the agency's poster child. I did not grow up dancing, not in dance studios anyway. I didn't find my way into a dance studio until I was almost 30, but I've spent years dancing over numerous kitchen floors and through the cycles of my life—most often unseen and unwitnessed. Movement has never been a social experience for me; it is has been a lifeline, a canoe carrying me along a spiritual migration.

Movement has always provided relief. So, when two young children, a struggling marriage and a challenging financial situation created more anxiety than I could manage, I turned to what I knew. I started taking classes in modern technique, improvisation, authentic movement and creative movement. My movement studies were not about steps, fitness, strength or flexibility; they were a pathway to self awareness. The movement provided a powerful grounding tool that allowed for expressive release, mind/body integration and emotional connection. As Development Director, I see it as my responsibility to create these opportunities for others.

It's a big job about which I have big passion. This work is important to me. But I really have no idea how to do it. My background is in magazine journalism. I was going to be a foreign correspondent, specializing in United States-Chinese relations. I spent my last year of college at the Chinese University of Hong Kong, learning Mandarin and studying international communications. And now here I am in Fort Wayne, Indiana working as a non-profit administrator. What do I know about modern dance? About non-profit development? About grant writing? The first grant I wrote was the one that partially funded this position–and I only *helped* write that one for goodness' sake, not like I did it all by myself.

But I am learning, fueled by enthusiasm. I am holding my own and more. I am growing. I am also pursuing a Master of Arts in dance/movement therapy. Only seven schools across the country offer the program, including Columbia College in Chicago. So I am commuting back and forth to school in Chicago while working and parenting and living in Fort Wayne. My life is a little crazy.

These calls I get from Mother about Daddy not feeling well seem to exist out there somewhere. As if Mom and Dad are orbiting around the sun of my solar system that is my kids, work and graduate school. But the calls become more frequent. And Daddy doesn't show any improvement. And I start listening more closely. I start hearing about frequent trips to the emergency room and my concern grows.

The entire family is planning to rent a van and travel together to Lexington, Kentucky for my cousin's wedding, but Daddy is having problems breathing so they take him to the doctor (again). The doctor sends him for a chest x-ray and discovers he has a collapsed lung. They remove fluid from his chest, put in a chest tube and inflate it. Needless to say, none of us will be going to the wedding in Kentucky.

Instead, my sisters, Babs and Lita, are coming here. Lita is a nurse who lives in Florida. Babs lives in Ohio and is a master at business related to banking and taxes and real estate and insurance... hallelujah! Let's get Babs and Lita up here. A nurse who loves us–that's what we need–and a master who can help us figure out what in the hell we should be doing. Someone who knows more about all this than I do because I can't quite see Daddy doing much dance/movement therapy.

Babs calls me at work to tell me they are transferring Daddy from the hospital in Huntington to the one in Fort Wayne where they will be doing a biopsy. "They wanted to take him in an ambulance," she explains, "but we said no. Mother and Lita and I are just going to drive him ourselves. So we'll meet you there."

Okay, I'll meet you there. I hang up the phone and look at it. Once, distracted, I answered the office phone saying, "Fort Wayne Dance Collective, this was Allison." The person on the other end of the line laughed and said, "It was? Well, who are you now?" Fortunately, it was a friend and we laughed about it. But that's how I feel right now. "Hello, this was Allison. Soon to be someone new."

I quickly finish what I'm doing. Actually, I leave it unfinished, but convince myself it's done well enough. And I leave. I get out of the office. I go to the hospital and wait. I imagine Mom and Babs and Lita racing over here. Mom doesn't navigate very well–especially when she's nervous. And Babs and Lita aren't very familiar with Fort Wayne. But I assure myself they'll find their way without mishap and arrive shortly.

I wait long enough for the waiting room's rhythms to become familiar. There is the ding of the elevator. There is the whoosh of the door. There is the hum of the TV and the undercurrent of quiet conversation and the phone ringing and the intercom calling doctors who walk around in scrubs looking haggard and worried and...where are they already? I look at the clock. I re-position myself to be certain that they must walk by me. (Could I possibly have missed them? Could I have possibly been so interested in this magazine that I let them walk by unnoticed?) I wait some more.

Finally, they arrive. Daddy is in his "non-jogging" suit and red plaid "jumper." He is walking slowly along the side of the hallway allowing faster people to brush by him. Tubes in his nose are attached to an oxygen tank that rolls beside him and he's carrying....what is that he's carrying? It looks like a clear, plastic, odd-shaped brief case. Babs and Lita and Mother are behind him carrying bags from Taco Bell.

"You stopped at Taco Bell?" I ask incredulously.

"Well, yes," Lita laughs.

"We were hungry!" Babs echoes

"So we decided to get something to eat!" Mother says offhandedly.

Daddy rolls his eyes, but I can see he's hiding a smile. Okay, maybe this isn't so bad after all. I mean, if they have time to stop at Taco Bell, how bad can it be?

"What's that?" I ask, pointing to the plastic brief case.

"That's collecting drainage from his chest cavity," Mother says. I get on the elevator with my family, bags from Taco Bell and a plastic brief case that is collecting drainage from Daddy's chest cavity.

This isn't good...isn't good at all.

JAN
January 2000

Deep silence fills the house. There are no sports playing on TV. There is no hum from Hank's oxygen machine. There are no sounds of activity from the kitchen. No voices chatter through empty rooms. Friends and family have all gone. Hank has missed Christmas and the new millennium. I struggle to find a new rhythm.

And get water. It is bitter cold and the water treatment plant in our neighborhood has blown up. My tears are the only water running in this house right now. Hank is dead and I can't even flush a toilet. I head into town, but when I push the window washer fluid button in my car, nothing comes out. I drive to the car dealer and walk up to the service window.

"Can I help you?" asks some unsuspecting young man.

I burst out crying and hear myself say, "I live in the Norwood sub-division and we don't have any water and I can't flush my toilet and my husband died and now my window washer fluid won't come out!" I am sobbing and can hardly talk or breathe.

The poor young man says, "Ma'am, we can fix your car. Go sit in our lounge and have a cup of coffee or a coke and just try to relax."

I go inside and sit in a nice, soft, comfortable chair and try to get my sobbing under control. "Good grief," I think. "I have lost my mind. I am acting like an insane person. I have to get a grip. That poor young man!"

With my windshield washer fluid now pumping freely, I drive home and take the Christmas tree down by myself. Everything takes such effort. I am overwhelmed by dirty laundry and decorations that need to be put away…and his empty chair. Our granddaughter recognized Hank at her wedding reception in November by marking an empty chair with a white bow. I sat by that empty chair and watched those two young people start their lives together. I hoped their love and marriage would grow to be as solid as ours was. When did I become this person watching the children of my children from the view of an empty chair?

"You were right," I think. "It must have been easier for you to die than for me to learn to live without you." You encouraged me to build a new life for myself and be happy. I'm trying, but it is so much harder that I anticipated. Nothing is normal. And I love normal. I have never liked adventure. But now normal has been attacked by this wild animal called grief and minor things rattle its cage. A lady my age was waiting at the door of a restaurant. A man came in and their eyes lit up when they saw each other. They kissed and grief lunged at me. When put on hold while making a business call, the song "When A Man Loves A Woman" started playing. Grief lunged again. I see couples holding hands and it pierces my heart. It's not just that I miss being part of a couple, I miss being part of a couple with Hank. I miss who he and I were together.

I long for life before April 1998, before we got cancer. Before cancer taught me how brave and adaptable he was. How sweet and tender and loving he could be even while enduring so many awful things. Before I discovered how strong I could be–how, with God's help, I could do things I never dreamed. Before I learned how far one can go on the little word hope. Before I learned that the human body never runs out of tears.

"You taught me well, my soul mate, lover, friend," I whisper to the silence. "I love you enough to let you go. I love you enough to redefine myself and find a way to fill this emptiness with joy." But first, I must wade through so much sadness. I must find my way across slippery rocks if I am to be part of this river of life that keeps flowing by me.

I wake at 3 a.m. thinking someone is pounding on my front door. Of course no one is there. But morning is the hardest time of day. I wake each day and remember Hank's dying as if it is a brand new feeling–as if it just happened. Raw, hard, painful, it is a feeling of drowning. I remember when Mother died suddenly in 1979 and we all gathered in Kentucky. I remember hearing the sobs coming from each bedroom early every morning as it hit each of us like a slap in the face as we woke: "she's dead." That's what I'm experiencing now. It's like my mind can't grasp it all at once. As if I need to be reminded anew each morning until I can finally wrap myself around the truth of his death.

The day is bitter and cold. The world is frozen and I am tired all the time. I have no desire to do anything or go anywhere. I have always been tense about driving–especially to new places. Now everywhere is new. I force myself to pick up the phone. "Hey, Don. I thought maybe I'd come and visit you and Jan later today." Maybe it will help, spending time with Hank's best friend. We were all such good friends.

"How's Jan feeling?" I ask. "Is she up to a visit?" Now Don's wife, Jan, has breast cancer and they are beginning their own cancer journey. "Okay then, I'll see you this afternoon." I already wish I wasn't going.

Their home is filled with the telltale signs of cancer–medicine bottles and tubes and machines. But they share it together. I feel so sad. Jan shows me a photo album she made for Don's retirement. There is, of course, a picture of Hank and Don. I cry, but only once, only once during the whole two hours; it's a new post-Hank record.

I go home cold, depressed and sleepy. I curl up with the heating pad and nap. When I wake up, I am still cold. I am too awake to sleep, but too sleepy to get up. My grief is so physical, I ache. My fibromyalgia attacks me with a vengeance though it was gentle with me through the months of Hank's illness and death. Now that my body is busy relearning how to breathe and eat and sleep, it is no longer able to protect itself.

I ache for Hank's hands holding mine or rubbing my back and shoulders. I long for his arms to embrace me in a hug. I miss our feet touching as we sat in our recliners. I miss lying next to him in the narrow hospital bed. I miss his face, his eyes, his mouth. I miss his loving, encouraging, helpful words. I miss his wisdom and companionship.

I don't want him to be just a memory. I believe Hank still feels and thinks with his spirit body. But knowing his spirit is free and off on a beautiful journey does not soothe my aching heart. I finally doze off and see him sitting across the room from me, wearing his navy and yellow striped short-sleeved shirt. He looks happy, healthy and relaxed. He is smiling and says, "I love you." I wake up and try to hold on to the dream.

I grieve in increments as if God will only allow me so many tears at a time to prevent my drowning. Just a little while ago I was sobbing and hurting so badly I thought I might die, but now I am calm. I go to the library and check out books about grief and loss. Books by professionals about the grieving process. Books by everyday people about their personal experiences. True stories of love and faith and ministry and learning to live again. All I want to do is read and nap. I feel drained and try to be gentle with myself. No pushing. If something feels too hard, I don't do it. I do what feels right for me, not what someone else wants or expects or thinks I should do.

Hank's brother calls. His voice sounds so much like Hank's it makes me cry. My girls call crying, caught in their own pain. The storm of death has passed through and left us all shattered in its wake– it's hard for us to help each other. Daddy and I go to lunch. Our small talk doesn't include things that matter. Is he missing Hank? Is he grieving? He doesn't acknowledge or share feelings. I can't find a way to connect with him while swimming in all this grief. I have never been a good swimmer. One summer, while I was taking swimming lessons, Cammie was being certified as a lifeguard. She had to jump in and save me three times in a single afternoon while I was practicing in a neighbor's pool. After the third time, she asked me to please just stay out of the water, or at least stay in the shallow end….now there is no shallow end. I am in way over my head and there is no lifeguard on duty; I must save myself.

HANK

*(letter to Jan written 5-20-1980
while traveling on business)*

Dear Jan,

I get off another plane, rent another car, drive down another dark road to another strange town.

I check into another empty motel room and turn on another TV.

I am alone with the memory of you and the assurance of our love.

Your touch makes the world quiet and brings me peace.

At the same time, it arouses the animal in me and makes me glad I am a man and you are my woman.

The physical pleasure you give me by being a little bit wicked and a whole lot of a woman soothes me.

Only a fool would leave a woman like you and travel from town to town.

Someday, soon I hope, I will be able to change this demanding travel schedule and stay by your side forever.

Until then, please continue to be my harbor in this storm, a place I can come to with the assurance that I am safe and secure.

Love,
Hank

JAN
January 2000

It's mid-afternoon and I am still in Hank's pajamas. I haven't showered or brushed my teeth. I haven't left the house. I read grief books and cry. My eyes are swollen and burn. My shoulders hurt. I have a throbbing headache. It takes so much energy to breathe. I am walking through the valley of the shadow of death. I make a list of important information and put it in Hank's desk for the girls in case I die. That's what Hank did for me. He was always the responsible one. Now I need to do the same for my girls.

If it weren't for my family, I wouldn't care if my life ended tonight. But I can't depend on family and friends to make me happy or help me build a new life. That has to come from within. I am a small ship launched onto an unknown sea of change. Hank had the courage to fight for his life. I must find the courage to fight for mine. I must find the courage to sail to this foreign, unknown land of widowhood trusting I will once again find peace and joy.

I gather sentimental things that remind me of Hank. I add a candle and create a sacred place. It comforts me to light the candle and spend quiet time there reflecting each evening. I continue to try and think of five things I am thankful for every day. In the mornings, I reassure myself by saying affirmations in a mirror:

"Jan, I love you.
You are going to be okay.
Whatever you need will come to you.
Just breathe."

I try to believe it. I am tired of all this crying and weary of this heavy load of grief. I decide to escape the winter and go to Florida. When Hank was getting treatment in Florida, our daughter Lita and her husband Ken bought a house with an in-law suite. Our eldest daughter, Babs, helped them find it while she was there visiting. Thinking we had beat the cancer and would need to get Hank's one lung out of the harsh Indiana winters, we had the in-law suite renovated to accommodate a wheelchair and oxygen tanks. He died before seeing the finished apartment. I thought it might be better that he had not lived here with me—but it's not. I can't feel him here like I do in Indiana. It is the first time in many years that we have had different addresses. My life has become one long fill in the blank: the first time I _____ without Hank.

HANK

(letter written 4-19-1980 while traveling)

Jan,

   Today while driving along Florida's Gold Coast, I see beautiful scenery.

   Some scenes look like postcards, yet they are sterile and lack something.

   After several such scenes flash by me like a travelogue, I realize what is wrong: the scenery is beautiful, but the soul is missing because there is no one to share it with.

   It is not the scenery that is the problem, it is me.

   I have an emptiness inside that I cannot fill by myself.

   Only you can fill that void and make me whole.

I love you,
Hank

JAN
February 2000

I can't bear to think of everything I will experience without Hank. The rest of my life is too big. I can only deal with this aloneness in tiny little pieces—one hour or one day at a time. I miss him–his body, our closeness, our intimacy, the completeness of who we were together. I don't want to survive him—but some unseen force keeps me putting one foot in front of the other, breathing in and out, getting up and going to bed, marking the days off the calendar.

I think about when Hank and I were young and dating and he broke up with me. It was 1955 and my friends and I all dreamed about getting married, starting families and being wives and mothers. Few of us talked about going to college. But I didn't dream of marrying somebody, someday…I dreamed of marrying Hank. We met when we were freshman in high school and began dating soon after. Hank was fun and dependable and trustworthy and hardworking. He was on the basketball team and the football team and the student council. He was voted most likely to succeed. It was so easy to fall in love with him! And even easier for him to break my heart.

"I think we're getting too serious," Hank said one night while we were out on a date. It was the fall of our junior year of high school. We had been dating for two years. "I think we need to go out with other people for a while and see how we feel."

I couldn't believe what I was hearing! And I had absolutely no idea how I should respond. I couldn't begin to find words that might even come close to making any sense. All possible voices of reason were silenced by the ringing in my ears and the pounding in my chest. The best I could do was murmur, "Okay."

"I'll still take you home after school," he suggested.

"I don't think that's a good idea," I managed to say, my thoughts scrambling. How could it possibly be a good idea for me to sit next to him or be alone with him or casually talk with him about his day if he is going to be dating someone else?

Instead, I watched from a distance as he started going out with one of the cheerleaders. I had a couple of dates with other people, but wasn't very interested. It was everything I could do to move through one day after another. Somehow, in spite of my lethargy, time moved on. Christmas lights eventually replaced the colored fall leaves and then Christmas vacation was over and I was back at school and the winter basketball season had started. Finally, the phone rang.

"We need to talk," Hank said.

"I don't know what we have to talk about," I answered. "I'm barely getting over this and don't want to get things stirred up again."

"Janice, we need to talk," he insisted.

Mother and Daddy had company over for dinner. I could hear the quiet conversation and the rattle of forks and knives against plates coming from the next room. I didn't want to interrupt their meal to ask if I could go out with Hank. Besides, they knew how upset I'd been about all this. They probably wouldn't think it was a good idea for me to see him. They probably wouldn't even allow him to come over. So I decided not to say anything. I just waited and watched out the window. When Hank's car pulled up I yelled, "I'm going out with Henry!" and ran out the door.

I got in the car and sidled up against the passenger door wondering what we could possibly have to talk about. Was he going to tell me how happy he was, what a good time he'd been having with his new cheerleader friend? Was he going to talk about the basketball team and his upcoming game? Was he going to talk to me about his college plans or ask me about my grades? He pulled the car over. I could feel him looking at me, but I didn't trust myself to meet his gaze. Instead, I stared at the dashboard and scrunched my shoulders up so I could sink down into my warm coat like a turtle pulling into its shell.

"Janice, you're in my skin," he finally said. "You're in my heart." My eyes filled with tears. "You're in my life and I can't get you out." I finally turned my head to look at him. " If you take me back, I'll never break your heart again," he continued. "I'll be yours forever."

"What about the other girl you've been dating?" I asked.

"Well, I have a date with her tomorrow night, but I'll call her and cancel it."

"No," I said. "I think you should keep the date and tell her in person. It's too hard to hear something like that on the phone. Now please take me home."

The next night I went to the basketball game and sat with my friends up high in the bleachers. Before the game, Hank came out in uniform. He walked across the gym floor and handed something to one of the kids sitting in the first row of bleachers. That person turned and handed something to the person behind him who turned and handed it to the person behind him and on and on until everyone was watching as the person in front of me turned and put something in my hand. It was Hank's student council pin. He and everyone else watched as I pinned it to my blouse, a public gesture that affirmed our private conversation–Hank and I were back together.

When I was a girl, I survived being separated from Hank after knowing the joy of his love. Will I survive now that I'm a grown woman? It has been 85 days since he died. And I still hate this new world of widowhood. It makes me feel like an outcast, out of step with society. I am not alive, but I am not dead; I feel disconnected. What lessons will I learn from this? What new songs will I sing? Will I be able to share this experience with others—to help other widows or widowers as they limp out onto their new journey?

CAMMIE
Memory 1998

Finally, we have a diagnosis. Mesothelioma? I don't believe it. The family asks questions and we discuss it with the doctor and each other. There are a lot of unknowns. I remember what I read. Mesothelioma, not associated to smoking. Almost always caused by exposure to asbestos.

"Daddy, when were you exposed to asbestos?" I ask.

"Must have been when I worked at the tire factory," he says.

Babs and Lita head to the library and I head back to my computer. Mesothelioma. A rare, aggressive form of cancer. May not appear until 30 to 50 years after exposure. The onset of symptoms is gradual and a person often experiences symptoms for four to six months before the diagnosis is made. Malignant cells develop in the protective lining that covers most of the body's internal organs. Its most common site is the outer lining of the lungs and chest cavity, but it may also occur in the lining of the abdominal cavity or the sac that surrounds the heart.

An aggressive form of cancer. Limited treatment options. Poor prognosis. The more I read, the greater my sense of urgency. I can't believe I've let months go by only half listening. There has to be something. Daddy once told me his investment in my college education was an investment in his own future. I dig deeper, determined to give him a dividend return. Overnight, I create a horizontal file organized by topic: disease; symptoms and diagnosis; treatment options; issues of litigation. I'm building a case all right, but not for the courts. I am urging my parents to take swift, decisive action.

The next morning we are all at the kitchen table, going over the file. I feel like a drama queen, hoping I am unnecessarily exaggerating things, convinced I am not. I have printed out information on two cancer centers that have had some success treating mesothelioma. I only found two. One is in Houston, Texas and the other is in Tampa, Florida.

I urge Mom and Dad to call them both. Today. Now.

"But we have an appointment with the oncologist in Huntington tomorrow," they point out. "We should at least hear what he has to say." That makes complete logical sense, to everyone at the table. But from what I've read, I know it's just protocol. If this doctor is able to treat mesothelioma successfully, he would be somewhere doing it. And getting a lot of attention for doing it. Because he's from here, we would have probably read about him in the local paper; he'd be a local icon or something. At the very least, I would have read about him through my research. He would not be a nameless face hidden in the bowels of a medical facility in some small town in Indiana.

I catch Daddy's eye as I slide the file across the table. "Read this, okay?" Mother is sitting beside him, but I can't look at her.

"Okay," he says and I go home.

We all go to the oncologist the next day. The doctor describes a course of treatment that not surprisingly makes no sense to me since it's full of words I've never heard—but that in itself concerns me. I don't hear any of the words I read about when researching successful treatment. It's not like there was a wide range of treatment recommendations–some of this should sound vaguely familiar and it doesn't. I try to ask intelligent questions, using the information I've learned as background, but of course I know just enough to sound dangerously ignorant. I'm talking myself in circles. And considering I am desperate to discredit this man and get us out of here, I'm also on the verge of sounding rude and that isn't helping.

Daddy zeroes in on the crux of the matter. "How much experience do you have treating mesothelioma?" he asks. "How many patients have you treated?"

"I've treated many mesothelioma patients," the doctor reassures him. "And many of them are doing well."

We all look at each other. We no longer have to discredit him; he's just discredited himself. Mesothelioma. A rare form of aggressive cancer. Limited treatment options. Poor prognosis. We all thank him and Mom and Dad head to Houston.

Their experience there isn't much better. The doctor in Houston basically tells them to go home and get his affairs in order. So they head to Tampa. And find hope. A doctor there is performing radical, but successful surgery. Daddy is run through a series of tests to determine if he would be a good surgical candidate. We wait. Surgery is approved and scheduled. They have three weeks to come home and get back to Florida for the procedure. They expect to be there about two weeks. And then this will all be over and we can put this whole experience behind us! We are all concerned, but excited. I feel a huge sense of relief.

This is a man I watched remove a stump from the front yard, roots and all, by tenaciously chipping away at it with a hand axe. This is a man who spent 10 years plodding through a four-year college degree with a wife, two jobs and three kids in tow. He survived three daughters for goodness sake – all he needs is a fighting chance, a strategy, a plan of action. He's due a return on his investment.

JAN
February 2000

Through 42 years of marriage, Hank encouraged and supported me. Even through the last week of his life, he continued making me feel like I could do anything. He told me over and over how much he had loved me through the years and that he had always been faithful. He thanked me for fighting with him and helping him through his long illness.

In the final weeks of his life, as it became clear that he was caught in death's downward spiral, he called Babs and asked her to go buy me a nice-sized diamond ring and bring it with her the next time she came. He said he wanted to replace the small diamond he had bought me years ago. The weekend he died, Hank asked me to call our minister neighbor, Carl, down to the house. With our three girls surrounding us, I sat with Hank on his hospital bed as Carl led us through the renewal of our vows. But this time there was no "until death do us part." Hank slipped this new diamond ring on my finger, said he'd always loved me and vowed to love me beyond death. He then encouraged me to go on without him, to feel free to build a new relationship and have a good life. He said he was sorry he wouldn't be with me during my dying time, but assured me he would be there waiting for me on the other side.

Later that weekend, when his pain became too great, the hospice nurse suggested we start morphine. She explained that if she did we would probably never get to speak to one another again. He nodded and whispered, "I love you." How sweet is the memory of those last words.

I compare this memory with that of our wedding day. We pretended we were going to school as usual, but instead we drove to Corinth, Mississippi. We stopped at a dime store and Hank bought me a ring and then we stopped at a service station and put on the dress clothes we had stashed in the trunk. We drove on to the courthouse and walked by some old men who were playing checkers. We started to ask them where the office for the Justice of the Peace was located, but before we could even get the words out they pointed down the hall without even looking up. Apparently kids in dress clothes had asked them this question before.

On the way down the hall we nervously practiced our made up birthdays. I was only 16 and Hank was 17 so we prepared to lie about our age. Ends up, in 1957 the Justice of the Peace was an old man named Homer who didn't seem to care that I nervously stuttered out a birthday that didn't make any sense. Nor did he seem to mind that Hank had inconveniently left his identification in the car with his wallet. We signed papers and started the proceedings.

"Do you, Henry, take this woman..." Homer began, "to have and to hold…"

"I do," Hank blurted out.

Homer paused and looked out at Hank over eyeglasses that slipped down his nose. He said, "Not yet," and continued. "…for richer, for poorer…"

"I do," Hank interrupted.

"Not yet," Homer said again. "…in sickness and in health, to love and to cherish from this day forward…"

"I do," Hank said yet again.

"Not yet," Homer repeated in patient monotone.

I guess Hank really did want to get married because he ended up saying "I do" four times before Homer finally got to the end.

"… until death do you part. Now," Homer said and looked at Hank.

"I do," Hank said for the last time, pulled out the ring and put in on my finger. It was so big, I had to hold up my hand with my fingers standing straight up in the air; if I put my hand down, my wedding ring would fall right off.

When the officials were over, Hank asked Homer, "What do I owe you?"

"Whatever you think it's worth," Homer said.

Hank reached into his pocket, pulled out the wallet that he had supposedly left in the car and handed him a single dollar bill. I was so embarrassed!

"Is that all you think it was worth?" I asked him as we walked back out into the hallway.

"Well, I only had $5 and I figured we'd need $4 for gas and lunch on the way home," he said. "So all I had left to give him was $1!"

All of a sudden I thought of the prom dress I had on layaway. "Maybe this is a good time for me to tell you I owe money on a prom dress!" I said worriedly, realizing that we were now legally responsible for each other's debts.

We walked back by the old men as husband and wife, newly weds already in debt. I was still holding my left hand straight up to keep my new ring from falling off. On the way home, we stopped by a service station and true to his word Hank bought gas and lunch: two slices of bologna, some crackers and two bottles of Pepsi. We found a place to sit outside in the shade and ate our celebratory wedding feast, then got in the car and went home. We didn't tell anyone that we were married. We were afraid that if they knew, they would have it annulled. So we lived separately and went on dates and talked on the phone and continued on as juniors in high school as if nothing had happened.

"Son, can you explain to me why you put on this job application that you are married?" Hank's dad asked him one day in early summer. He caught Hank off guard as he was coming out of the shower. Hank had been having problems finding a job so he finally checked the married box on a job application hoping it would help. His brother saw the application lying on Hank's desk and asked him about it and their Dad overheard the conversation. He now wanted to hear Hank explain firsthand. So he did. He told the truth, though I imagine he left out all the details about Homer and the too-big ring and the old men. Once the story was out his dad said, "I'll give you a week to tell Janice's parents and if you don't, then when the week's up I'll go over and tell them myself."

I waited out the week and finally told Mother and Daddy on the last day. There was no yelling, no hysterics; there didn't even seem to be much surprise—just simple acknowledgement by both sets of parents that if we were married, we should be living together. So we moved back and forth, spending one month living with my parents and the next month living with his parents…and just in the nick of time because as it ended up I had become pregnant; our first baby was due in January.

Once my pregnancy started showing, I was not allowed to attend high school—even though I was blissfully married. Hank and my Dad went to a school board meeting and asked if I could please finish school and get my diploma. The school board allowed me to complete a correspondence course from home. Babs was born in January and we took her to the senior prom in the spring. Hank and I both graduated, but I was not allowed to go across the stage in a robe and gown; I was given my diploma in the gym without pomp or circumstance. But Hank was there with Babs and I was happy.

I am hungry for Hank and my old life, but I challenge myself to feel grateful. If Hank and I had never tasted love, if I had not felt so full, my loss wouldn't be nearly so palpable. I am reminded of a quote by George Eliot:

"What greater thing is there for two human souls
than to feel they are joined for life—
to strengthen each other in all labor,
to rest on each other in all sorrow,
to minister to each other in all pain,
to be with each other in silent unspeakable memories
at the moment of the last parting?"

I may always crave Hank's touch, his smell, his love, but with time my hunger and thirst will subside. This knowing is what keeps me from curling up in a ball and staying in bed in a darkened room.

Today I am going to lunch. I get dressed and look in the mirror to put on lipstick. I am shocked by my reflection. Widowhood and grief are ugly, ill-fitting garments. The color isn't right and the lines and style are all wrong. They highlight the sadness in my eyes and accentuate my wrinkles. They are the two most unbecoming, most uncomfortable things I have ever worn. But for now, nothing else fits. I wear them in private and public. This is how I present myself to the world. I hope in time the color will soften, the lines will flow and be less rigid and will become more flattering.

Maybe cultures that allow grieving people to wear sack cloths and ashes and scream and wail and tear their clothing are smarter than we are. At least a black armband would announce to the world, "My beloved husband is dead. I am a widow. Life as I knew it is over. I hurt." When I am out in a crowd, I want my pain to be seen. But it is invisible. I don't scream or wail or tear my clothes. I conform and go silently and sadly about the business of living, cloaked in this ugly wardrobe of grief that the world doesn't notice.

Nothing feels right anymore. Happiness is fleeting—it floats in on gossamer wings and then it's gone. When I am here in Florida, I miss family in Indiana. When I am in Indiana, I miss family in Florida. I am always missing someone who is somewhere else and now I miss Hank all the time. It is time to go back home to our empty house in the woods in Indiana.

CAMMIE
Winter 2000

It catches my eye from across the room—a small picture with bright colors against a dark background. As I get closer, I see a clothesline strung between bandaged trees with men's and women's and children's laundry being tossed chaotically by a frenzied wind. The blackened sky rains blood and lightning flashes through the middle of the stormy picture. I am captivated by its emotion. It is only because I stand staring for so long that I finally notice the words around the frame, written in a color that is barely perceptible: "An individual doesn't get cancer, a family does."

I fall onto a nearby bench and sob. After watching Daddy slowly debilitate over a long period of time, I am now struggling to accept his death. Trying to maintain some sense of normalcy, I have joined my daughter's class for a field trip to the local art museum. And there I have found my grief pictorialized.

Daddy is dead. This new truth is still settling in. Jacob, India and I have returned to our lives. We go to work, we go to school. We go to karate and violin and the dentist and the grocery. . . . . . it catches up with me at the grocery. Since Mom and Dad's return from Florida, we have spent so much time at their house that I haven't bought real groceries in months. Standing at the check out, watching the cashier scan the many items it takes to keep a household alive, it becomes real. Things have changed. He is gone. My budding grief bursts into full bloom and I start sobbing. The poor cashier asks if I found everything I was looking for... unable to speak, I nod through my tears, clumsily pay and leave, much to everyone's relief. Grief is certainly messy and inconvenient.

I am grateful for a flexible schedule that allows for such grief. During the past six months, trying to accommodate grad school and Daddy's illness, I have quit two jobs. The first was my beloved seven-year position as the Development Director of the Fort Wayne Dance Collective.

But it was as demanding as the cancer, so I let it go. The next was a position as a Movement Therapist at a psychiatric hospital–a unique opportunity to practice new skills while still a student. But working independently as a contracted grant writer was the only job that allowed me the time I wanted with my parents. Since spring, the kids and I have visited Mom and Dad every weekend. For the last few months before his death, I went once a week and stayed with Dad while Mother ran errands. The kids and I evaluated our priorities and put our lives on hold. Not out of obligation, but joyously, with a vision of hope. In the end, it wasn't enough. In the last days Dad whispered to me with labored breath, "There's nothing more you can do."

I am inspired to do big art. I am gathering large cardboard boxes from furniture and appliance stores. Over the years, I have developed a body of three-dimensional, interactive collages. Seeking to integrate movement into this traditionally static media, my pieces have been hinged, layered and sculpted, but never has a piece been as big as what I am now motivated to create. Never has my sadness run so deep. And never has it boomed so loud.

In my absence, friends debuted the taiko drum at a performance last weekend. Few taiko drums exist in the Midwest. Most are on the West Coast, made out of wine barrels. But I deferred to my Kentucky heritage and brought 50-gallon bourbon barrels back from a Louisville distillery. Took us two years to make this first drum. No tools, no money, no space, no skills...sheer will and determination. My father's life epitomized. I finished it shortly after Mom and Dad returned from Florida. I called Daddy and excitedly said, "Listen, " and drummed into the phone. He heard it, but he never saw it. He never felt up to making the 45-minute trip from his house to mine. We've named this first drum "Hank" in his memory. When I told Mother, she cried. Big art, big drums, big grief. My heart bleeds.

And all-too-familiar spasms shoot up my neck. Every year, my body remembers what my mind does not. But this year, the annual rigidity hangs on longer than usual. On December 21, when I was 21 months old, I aspirated a straight pin into my left lung. Doctors attempted to remove it with a bronchoscope, but I went into convulsions; the medications they used to stop the convulsions sent me into a coma. I was transported to Memphis where the pin was surgically removed and I spent weeks fighting for my life. The journey is still visible, marked by a battle scar that travels from mid-chest to mid-back.

Dad and I found it ironic that, in the end, we shared the same scar. Mine around the left side from where they removed the pin; his around the right side from where they removed his lung. Some esoteric circle is now complete. Discussing this shortly before his death, we both cried in empathy for the other, for the painful struggle we each had to face—me at the beginning of my life, he at the end of his–a shared understanding that no matter how you slice it, when they cut into your lung it hurts. Thirty some years ago he stood bedside, watching helplessly as I eventually healed. A few months ago, I stood bedside watching helplessly as he slipped into the night.

I write this to myself. I sing it to the stars. I whisper it to the moon. I dance under a black sky raining blood on bare winter trees. I drum as cancer's windy rhythm rips my family from our clothesline of hope and tosses us chaotically through grief's storm. I cower from the full force of the gale and desperately hope for the strength to hold on.

JAN
February 2000

I am back in Indiana, buried in snow. Just like Hank who is buried in the ground. Still. No miracle of resurrection. I walk in the house and see him sitting in his chair by the fireplace. I see him lying in the front room after he died, wearing his plaid "jumper" over his pajamas, looking like he is asleep. In my mirage he is, of course, on his right side. After his lung was surgically removed, he could only lie on his right side. If he lay on his left side, he couldn't breath. How awful it must have been to only lie in one position. Especially when lying down was all he was able to do.

I realize I am not grieving for him—he is now better off. I am grieving for myself, selfishly so. I look back to the first days and weeks of his illness and realize how naïve we were. Some unseen sculptor began chipping away at pieces of our life that we would never get back. We thought the crumbling pieces were temporary. How wrong we were. We did not realize this unseen hand was forever changing the shape and angles of our very existence. We didn't realize it was carving us into some brand new form attached to an oxygen tank by an umbilical cord. He lost his hair, his strength, his ability to climb stairs—the only thing we got back was his hair. We exchanged everything else for intimate talks, cherished moments and time for understanding and acceptance of his imminent death.

Lita, Ken, Hank and I were sitting in the surgeon's office at the Cancer Center in Tampa when I first saw mesothelioma up front and personal. The doctor put the CT scan up on the light board and pointed to the malignant areas and explained exactly what he would do during surgery. The cancer was ugly and we wanted it out of him! The doctor assured us several meso patients had responded well and had lived five years after surgery. I thought, "Five years! Wow! That would be wonderful!" It's amazing how our perspective can change. Three months earlier, if someone had told me Hank would die in five years I would have been devastated. But at that moment, five years seemed like such a gift…our little spark of hope burst into a large flame.

The secretary gave us a surgery date for July. It seemed like such a long time to wait. I wished they could do it the next day. I remember how grateful I was that Lita and Ken were nurses and lived near Tampa so they would be near us through the surgery and the follow-up treatment. The four of us went to lunch after the appointment and were on such an emotional high…this doctor had given us hope and we were hanging on. After lunch, Lita and Ken took us to the airport. We were flying home so we could prepare to return in a few weeks for the surgery. Before long, the agent announced, "Ballard, party of two, please come to the desk. Your seats have been reassigned." Ballard, party of two. I was so aware of how important those words were. We hugged Lita and Ken and boarded the plane. We had a plan. We had a date. We were on our way! A party of two.

I remember another day at the end of our journey in October 1999 when Hank was much worse. I held him as he cried. "I don't know how to quit fighting," he said. "I don't know how to give up." I told him that he had met every challenge life had given him and he would meet this one too.

I said, "When each day is worse than the one before and you have no good days left, then you'll know it's time to give up." Then we held each other and cried together. Hank kept his nose to the grindstone his whole life. He worked hard, set goals, stayed on track and kept putting one foot in front of the other. He led a quality life; he maintained morals and found the grit and determination to see things through to the end. It just was not in him to give up and quit. But we had to learn that there is a time to fight and a time to yield. Hank had to learn how to succumb to his pain and suffering and we both had to learn to yield to his death.

I remember a night just a few weeks before he died. We'd had a difficult 24 hours. He was having trouble breathing and I was having trouble with the oxygen tank. We were both worn out. I had learned to nap when he slept, but he had not slept much the night before or that day. He was in pain and no food sounded good to him. Finally, we went to bed early. He was in his hospital bed in our living room and I was on the mattress on the floor beside him. I remember thinking for the first time "Hank is going to die." It was the first time I actually let the words form in my mind. I realized that after all he had been through and all I had done to stand between him and death, he was going to die. I was almost in a panic and was crying quietly. Fear and sadness wrapped around me like a quilt and I thought they might suffocate me.

I prayed and quoted some of the scriptures that I had turned to so often through our cancer journey and began to calm down. "Yes," I thought. "He is going to die. But he is not going to die tonight and not tomorrow and probably not this week. He is still here now, sleeping near me. I will NOT let the fear of his death steal one moment from me. I will deal with that when the time comes and not one minute before!" This was such a pivotal moment for me. Up until that moment I had used the words, "If he dies" or "If he were to leave me," but this was different. This was a deep knowing within my spirit and mind that Hank was indeed going to die and there was nothing I could do to prevent it.

Looking back, I am so grateful for the opportunity to have shared the cancer journey with him. So grateful he was not taken from me suddenly. So grateful for the many moments that helped us come to a place of acceptance. So grateful he had the courage to die slowly, to fight for his life and to then yield to death with grace and dignity….. now he is gone, buried under all this snow. I am the one still holding on. I pray for the courage, grace and dignity to let him go. To set him free.

It is my first Valentine's Day without Hank in 45 years. A year ago, we were so full of hope that our cancer battle was behind us and we were on the road to recovery. Hank gave me a beautifully matted, framed verse about angels. Lita made us dinner and took a beloved photograph; the love between us in that picture is as poignant as his bald head. This year I am alone, with no card or gift, no hug or companionship or hope, just memories and a promise to stand alone. I brace myself for his birthday. It brings with it a terrible ice storm; my world is frozen inside and out.

HANK

(written in 1964)

Love is the most beautiful bud
in the bouquet of human emotions
and only bursts into full bloom
when shared with another.

—by Henry A Ballard

JAN
March 2000

Spring whispers a promise of new beginnings, but I can barely hear its voice. I seem to either sleep too much or not enough. My days have no joy; there is no reason to look forward. I suppose I am depressed. I suppose anti-depressants might help, but I need to feel this pain. I don't want it masked by drugs. I have discovered my grief to be as solid as my love. I can't go over it or under it or around it—I have to chisel my way through and that is what I intend to do. Armed with nothing but my own resolve, I am in the midst of a healing process that will make me a stronger, better person if I survive. I will not be consumed by this sorrow; I will not hibernate from my future. I am determined to emerge.

But it is so overwhelming. Clutter is everywhere. I can't seem to bring any order to these remnants of my previous life, of Hank's illness, of his death, of my months of travel and immobility. Little by little, I try to organize the chaos. I plow through the hopelessness. Sometimes I eat. On a rare day, I cook. In an even more rare moment, I go into Hank's study. His T-shirt is on the floor. It says, "Tough times don't last–tough people do." Hank was tough. He lived hard and fought hard and he died. I sob. I'm not tough. I can't do this. It's too hard. After Hank died I wrote, "I am not afraid of this grief–but ready to embrace it, flow with it, learn from it, work through it and become whole." Well, I am afraid of it now. It's bigger and blacker than I expected.

I take his picture to bed, hold it close and sob harder. I want to crawl into a dark hole, curl up and stay there. Instead, I get up and try to focus on the positive things in my life. Our anniversary is coming. Another first to get through. I look forward to getting through a day without crying. I hope it comes before my body breaks.

A friend spots Cammie and the kids and me out having lunch. She says we look awful. She sees us wearing the shared garment of grief that weaves between family members when a loved one is lost. She sees it, but she doesn't recognize it; she doesn't know its face or its name. She still has her mate. All my friends still have their mates, except for one acquaintance who was married as long as Hank and I. Her husband died a week after Hank did. She is getting married in a few months. I certainly don't see anything wrong with her remarrying, but I can't imagine being in a new relationship. I can't even imagine being able to eat in public without everyone around me tasting my sadness. A lot of people don't seem comfortable around me. They don't seem to know what to do with me, this new widow, this broken shard. They don't know how to help relieve my pain. I don't blame them. I don't know what to do with me either.

I remember my friend, Jean, calling in December after Hank died saying she wanted to come help me with anything I needed. I asked her to help me put up the Christmas tree. (If it weren't for the little kids I wouldn't have put one up at all, but with her help I did it. How sweet of her to have offered such a gift!) She arrived at 9 a.m. the next day. She helped me bring in all the boxes from the garage and helped me put the tree up and decorate it. I decided to put the tree in a different place and I think that helped. Change is good. Anything to break up the memory of how things were. I cried and asked her if she would please put the angel on top–that was always Hank's job. Then she helped me set the village out under the tree. As she left, she told me she was coming back the next day to deep clean any room. She arrived the next morning with her arms full of cleaning supplies. I asked her to clean the living room, the room Hank died in. Boy did she clean! Baseboards, walls, windows, furniture…everything smelled so fresh and clean when she was finished! What a precious gift she gave me. And she left me a ladder–one that I can manage alone. I cried again. I hate being so needy.

My grandson makes the varsity soccer team. My daughter gets a new job. My friends have new grandchildren. Life ambles on. I wake up to hear the peaceful sound of the rain hitting the windows and my first thought is, "Why get up? No one is here and no one is coming." I don't seem to care about anything. I force myself out of bed. I reach out to friends and family. I allow myself time alone. I dream about sex. I mechanically perform the tasks of daily living.

As the daffodils and tulips that Hank planted begin sprouting, so does my anger. The whole earth is coming alive, but Hank is still dead. Spring brings a whole new array of things to remember and miss. I miss the dirt he would bring in from the garden. I miss the way the smell of the earth would cling to him. I sit out on the screened porch to enjoy the weather and remember him saying, "We have a good life, don't we? Aren't we lucky we still love each other?"

I want to honor that life and that love. I want to enjoy the light of a new day and the fresh color of blooming flowers and the soothing sound of the rain. He is missing these things and I want to experience them for both of us. I want to be happy again and I have no idea how. I am worried about taxes. I am worried about bills. I am worried about spring yard work. I get a letter from the neighborhood association asking if my water meter is working–I have no idea–I don't even know where my water meter is. These are all things Hank took care of. I feel so dumb.

I call the CPA. I ask a friend to show me where the water meter is. I call a lawn service and realize I may have to get a new lawn mower, one that is lightweight and easy to start. (Maybe I'll get a pink one!) I join a friend for dinner and a movie. I go to the dentist. I do some cross-stitch. I open windows and let warm spring air blow through the house. I clean out closets. I make a lot of trips up and down the stairs and feel tired in a good way. The house is cleaner than it has been since Hank got sick. It feels good to get things done, but I still can't make myself work in his study. I get legal and financial things in order for the girls in case something happens to me. The lady at the bank says I have to open a new checking account in my name only. I feel a little more in control, but also like I am getting rid of a little more of Hank all the time.

One of our "couple" friends calls and invites me to their new house for dinner and out to the symphony. My first feeling is fear. I am afraid of driving at night. I am afraid of not being able to find their new house. I am afraid of finding my way back home late at night. I am afraid of being solo in the company of a couple. But I accept the invitation. I get directions, get dressed up and go. As I head out of town, I ask Hank to help me think clearly and find my way.

It is awkward being with them in their new house. The dynamics of all these old relationships has changed. Without Hank, we are like a car with three wheels instead of four. We bump along, trying to redefine our friendship. At the symphony, there is a couple sitting in front of us who is about our age. He puts his arm around her and pulls her close; she leans into him and he whispers in her ear. I cry quietly. I feel alone and continue crying all the way home, but I also feel strong and glad that I went.

HANK

(written October 1976)

Dear Jan,

   I thought I would take this opportunity to put in writing that I love you and was very proud of you last night at the party. You were the prettiest one there. Take care of yourself and I will see you soon.

Love,
Hank

JAN
April 2000

The month of March seemed to go on forever. I get up and feel ready to work in Hank's study. I go through the rest of his clothes and start going through the files in his desk. I only get through one drawer before I have to quit. He kept every card the girls and I ever gave him and it is hard to read them. It is hard to see his handwriting and his columns of numbers on the financial ledgers in his files. I only get through one drawer, but the task is started and I am proud of myself.

I do not feel joy, but am grateful to have some relief from such extreme sadness. I am rediscovering pleasure. I can look at the blooming daffodils and budding forsythia without crying. But the song "I Believe I Can Fly" seems to follow me wherever I go and always brings me to tears. It started playing while I was at the store making copies. I just kept making copies as if I were a normal person and not a crazy lady standing there crying. I no longer allow my tears to drive me out of stores or away from people. I have learned to do just about anything while crying.

Jacob and India are out of school for spring break so Cammie brings them to stay for a couple of days. We all walk down the road, into the woods and try to find the tree where Hank had carved our initials. Jacob goes to the yard and shoots the BB gun. I go out with him and we start talking about Hank and hold one another and cry.

I take the kids to the store and buy several large plastic storage boxes. I think I may be ready to organize the garage soon; the kids have offered to help. Looking at all the stuff in the garage overwhelms me. Just being in the garage overwhelms me. I can see Hank standing at his workbench–I can't be out there without crying. Maybe it will be easier with the kids' help.

I remember telling Cammie not long after Hank died that I didn't think it was good for Jacob and India to be around me as I cry so much. She said they need to know how we feel and see how we handle grief. They need to see us cry and then see us get better; she thinks it's important we let them see this grieving, healing process. Such a large teaching for such young souls.

CAMMIE
Spring 2000

I am standing in the bathroom looking in the mirror. I am exhaust-ed. I really don't know how much more of this I can take. My legs simply cannot hold my body up one more minute. I fall to the floor, sobbing and curl into fetal position. The kids hear me crying and come to see what's wrong. Well, let's make a list: I'm divorced, exhausted, over-worked, overextended and poor. I have no foundation, no sense of security, no shield protecting me from the world, no comfort, no relief and my dad is dead. I wanted to find a way to save him, but there was nothing I could do. I wanted to be a heroine and I'm not, so instead I am lying in a heap on the floor. Woman down; mother spent; wife dis-placed; daughter lost.

The kids are of course unsure of what to do or say. I feel India's hands as she comes in close. She drapes her little body over my back and hangs over me like a monkey in National Geographic. My sobs cause her to rise and fall as if I have become some sort of new amuse-ment park ride—one that is not very amusing. I see Jacob's dirty, untied tennis shoes through my blurred vision. Then I feel his hands on my head. "Mother, get up," he says.

The voice in my throat doesn't answer, but the voice in my head stubbornly refuses. I am never getting up again, I think. I am going to spend the rest of my life in this spot. Down here, close to the ground so I won't have very far to go when I fall.

"Mom, get up," he says again. This time I at least raise my head. From my low position, he seems about six feet tall. He squats in front of me, brushes my hair out of my eyes and says, "Mom, it's all right. Everything is okay."

"No, it's not," I answer. "Daddy Hank is dead and it will never be okay again." I sob harder. I hate myself for saying these words, for dar-ing to speak this truth. What kind of person am I that I would think this, much less say it? What kind of mother am I that I would say it to my children?

Jacob's shoulders shrug slightly. "Mom, it's okay. He's dead, but he's not. You know he's not." I look at him doubtfully. "We are a spiritual tribe," he continues. "We have all been together forever and will continue being together forever." He places his hands on my face, my shoulder, my arms, my back. "This is not who we are," he says. "These bodies are not what tie us together." He puts my hand on his heart. "This is who we are. This is what connects us and that's not going to die. That's never going to change."

I search his face. Who is this person? This child I've birthed and raised and loved, who is he? I have nothing to say in response. There are no words. Jacob stands and pulls me up. I rise, bringing India monkey up with me, still on my back. "How do you know that?" I ask.

He looks surprised. "From you," he answers and gestures at the family pictures hanging on a nearby wall. "I learned that from all of you."

I take a big, deep breath and smooth my rumpled clothes. Maybe, just maybe, I am not a terrible mother after all. Maybe, just maybe, I am strong enough to carry my family and myself through another moment, another day. Maybe, just maybe, we can find our way.

JAN
April 2000

I go through the basket Hank kept by his chair and find his wallet with his driver's license and cards. He has been dead 22 weeks, 154 days. I guess he doesn't need these things anymore. I wonder when I will stop counting the weeks, months and days. Our loss ripples into our future and expresses itself in countless ways. A male neighbor comes down and shows Jacob how to check the oil in the car and put in windshield wiper fluid and clean off the battery. Hank should be here to teach him these things. We hear that granddaughter Haley will be going to American University Law School in Washington, D.C. Hank would be so proud. He should be here to greet such good news.

Hank had to work so hard to get through school. He started attending college part time the fall after we graduated high school. Babs was already 8 months old. We were so young! When I became pregnant with Lita a few years later, we moved back in with Hank's parents to save on expenses. After she was born, he dropped out of school and worked as the manager of a bowling alley so we could afford to move out and live independently. When he was hired at the local rubber plant a year later, his benefits included tuition. He went back to school part-time and continued working full-time, determined to take care of his family and finish his degree.

He was always tired and often gone, but we were happy. I loved being married. I loved putting everything I had learned in my home economics class to good use. I always did like to sew and decorate and make things and play house. I loved doing these things even more as Hank's wife and Babs' and Lita's mother! Not only did I make most of the clothes the girls and I wore, I also made curtains and bedspreads and painted walls and refinished old pieces of furniture and re-upholstered the couch. I took a correspondence course in interior decorating and learned more about how to make each of our many rental houses beautiful, even on a budget.

And Hank continued finding ways to let me know how much he appreciated me, even though he was exhausted from working and going to school and even though we didn't have much money. He would pick bouquets of cattails from the side of the road and bring them home to me. And on Christmas when I was sick with the flu, he went to the grocery and came in grinning saying, "I have a Christmas surprise!" The girls and I were so excited! He reached into the bag and pulled out four little ice cream balls rolled in coconut with icing on top in the shape of holly leaves and little red candles waiting to be lit. What a treat! We just didn't have the money to spend on things like that! I was brimming with happiness. In spite of my fever and aching muscles. "Thank you Hank!" I said as I hugged him.

1n 1963 our third daughter, Cammie, was born and our family was complete. I was so grateful to be a stay-at-home Mom. I took care of the house and kids and Hank went to work and school and mowed the yard and took care of home repairs and the car. He didn't change diapers or get up with the girls at night or do laundry or cook dinner unless there was a specific need for him to do so. We worked well together as a team within our clearly defined roles and we hardly ever argued.

Hank finally graduated with a bachelor's degree in 1968. As the girls grew older, he grew as a Dad. He loved giving piggy-back rides and reading books. He never quite learned how to make the girls' favorite "chocolate" toast, but he did manage to sew the ears onto Cammie's beloved stuffed rabbit when they fell off. And when I became a Girl Scout Leader, he became a registered Girl Scout and went with us on troop camping trips. He taught the girls to build fires and ride bikes. We joined the country club and he took the girls swimming and coached softball teams. We lived and loved and worked and played and somehow the years just passed by. As we watched our girls grow up and get married and begin having babies of their own, I realized Hank and I weren't kids anymore; at some point, we had all grown up together.

I can hardly remember the person I was—or the life we had before cancer. I don't yet know this joyless woman I have become. Hank was still alive in the fall, and even though he wasn't doing well we were still enjoying one another and our home. Then he died, and my hope and spirit died with him. It's almost Easter. In my other life, I would be full of the joy of spring and excited about decorating my home for the holiday. I no longer decorate for the changing seasons. I don't feel I will ever regain all of me. I was too much a part of Hank for too long. We were entwined like the wood carving he once sculpted—one piece of wood with two heads, each of the two parts with flaws. He told me the carving was of us, two separate, imperfect individuals who came together to form one person—like conjoined twins who share one heart and can't live if separated. But we have been separated. Death has separated us. It proved to be the only thing that could keep us apart.

Now that we are apart, I have started thinking about what to do about the house. Part of me wants to stay here. I love the house and the woods and the memories of Hank that are here, but part of me thinks I need to get a smaller home with no steps, one that will be easier for me to manage as I get older. There are so many decisions to make and so many things that need attention. I go to WalMart and ask the car man to check the air in my tires. I'm scared to do it myself, though I don't know why. I hate having to learn all these things that Hank did. This new terrain I am walking seems vast and barren. I keep asking myself, "What can I learn from this experience? How can I grow?" Maybe I can learn to help others. I should probably learn to check my air pressure first.

I am caught on a roller coaster of good days and bad days. I try to work through my list, but some days I just don't have the energy or the focus. Yesterday I was driving and saw a man walking who was about Hank's age and size. He had grey hair like Hank and was dressed in jeans and a plaid, flannel, quilted jacket like Hank wore. I started crying so hard I almost had to pull the car over. Joann calls and says she dreamed our group of friends gathered together and Hank asked them to help me go on with my life. In the dream I thanked all of them and then pulled out a gun and shot myself. It upset her a lot and she is crying. I know my friends feel as helpless as I do. This grief has taken the normal ordinary days we used to share and turned my life into something unknown and unfamiliar.

Today is beautiful, sunny, in the 70s, no wind, birds singing, daffodils and tulips blooming. If Hank was here and well, he would work in the yard, then come in happy and dirty and sweaty. He would shower and watch a ball game. Instead, my new roommate, grief, hovers silently, a looming presence that demands attention, but offers nothing in return. It doesn't mow the yard. It doesn't weed the flowerbeds. Instead of encouraging and supporting me like Hank did, this new roommate challenges me and causes me to be uncertain, unsure. Right now I hate this house and am ready to sell it, but by tomorrow I will have changed my mind.

I am trying to learn to focus on simply moving through one day, one moment at a time. Today I have my prayer time in bed and decide to take charge. I call a man who advertised in the paper and ask him to come mow my yard. I call a young couple starting a landscaping business and ask them to come redo two large flowerbeds. I get the car serviced and buy a lilac bush, pansies, pine bark and mulch. I have a neighbor lift the bags out of the car for me. I do lots of yard work and get the hummingbird feeder out. I get a small fountain and am soothed by the noise of the moving water. I'm tired, but don't feel emotionally drained. It feels good to take control and make something happen. Maybe I'll figure out how to kick out my unwelcome roommate named grief.

HANK

(an original writing found in Hank's desk after his death)

The warm sun of spring shines on pure love.
Everyday is a perfect day filled with full yellow buttercups,
ice blue geraniums, blazing red roses and ivory white mums.
The flowers are there, but are we able to see them?
Do we realize what riches are ours for the taking
until we are shut up in a room with no access to the beauty?
When the beauty is gone,
we suddenly realize that there is a void,
that we are not a whole being.
Then and only then can we fully appreciate
what we have been freely given.

CAMMIE
Memories 1977 and 1999

The ball whizzes by about six feet from my head. "I'm right here!" I shout, "not over there!" I am 14 years old and playing catch with a member of my softball team. And this kid's aim, or lack thereof, is annoying. Every time she throws, the ball goes way over my head or off to the side out of reach. Dad, who helps coach my team, is watching. I run over for a drink of water. "I sure wish she would learn to throw!" I complain in frustration.

"Hmm." Dad says. "Seems like that's quite an opportunity she's throwing at you."

"Huh?" I ask taking off my hat and wiping the sweat off my face. I look up at him, squinting into the sun. I don't understand his point any better than I can see his face. What is he talking about? I ask myself as I run back for another round of expected torture.

Instead, everyone on the team is told to rotate. Every time my new partner throws, the ball lands right in my glove. The two of us fall into an easy rhythm of catch-step-throw, back and forth and back and forth. "This is more like it," I think. I love feeling the solid smack of the ball landing in the center of my glove. I love the moment of suspension as I land the catch on my back foot, then lunge forward. I love the stretch of release as my weight shifts, my arm whips out in front of me and my whole body propels the ball through the air.

"Good throw," Dad says as he walks up beside me. We are both proud of my arm that has developed slowly over the last few years after hours of playing catch together.

"Thanks," I say without losing my stride. Back and forth and back and forth. He's still standing there. "What?" I ask, sensing he has something to say.

"Well, I'm just noticing how much easier it is to catch that ball when it's thrown right at you," he says.

"Yeah', no kidding," I snicker.

"In fact, it's so easy, almost anybody could do it," he adds casually.

"Huh?" I break my rhythm and hold on to the ball, watching as he walks away. What does he mean anybody can do this? He knows better than anybody that it's taken me three years of practice to be able to effortlessly execute this complex series of movements with such precision. What is he talking about?

"Throw the ball!" my partner yells impatiently. Too late. The coach calls for another rotation. One of our newer team members steps into place across from me. "Here we go again," I think and send the ball flying over to her. Her return throw is way over my head. In a burst of frustrated energy I jump up and grab it.

"Wow! Good catch!" she yells across the grass as I lob the ball back to her. This cycle repeats. Determined to catch the ball, I run, jump, reach and dive, a puppet to her every erratic throw. It requires a ton of energy and focus, but surprisingly enough, I catch more than I miss. Even more surprising is how exhilarating it feels!

As the season continues, I discover that seasoned players who are able to actually throw the ball to me provide me a chance to smoothly, flawlessly catch and return with a satisfying rhythm. But the girls who erratically throw wild balls give me a chance to be a superstar! I start looking for chances to partner with less-skilled team members rather than avoiding them. My motives are not altruistic; I am pushing my skill level. I learn to jump behind, in front of, up to, or down on anything that flies, rolls or bounces anywhere near my proximity. I have learned that bad throws create the opportunity for great catches. I am positioned as shortstop and command the infield.

Years later, I am sitting in the hospital room in Florida watching Dad while Mother gets some sleep. The hospital's nightly routine provides a soothing background to the bad turn Dad's recovery has taken. He was doing so well after the surgery. (Well, except for that one time his heart went out of rhythm and his blood pressure dropped and they had to take him into surgery and use paddles and medicine to get things back to normal… other than that, he's been doing really well!) But then he started having problems breathing; severe enough that we have all gathered back in Florida to support him and Mother and each other as we wait to see what happens next.

Apparently, sometime between the bronchial spasms and the incompetent respiratory therapist, Daddy asked Babs to change a sentence in his will. Today was Good Friday and business offices were closed making it hard to do get much business done until Monday. But in the middle of a particularly awful bronchial spasm Dad looked my sister dead in the eye and said "go take care of this for me." So she spent the day on the phones trying to figure out how to handle it. And Lita monitored Daddy's vitals and the nursing staff to make sure they were all doing their jobs. And Buddy and Ken took all the kids out to find something to do that was more entertaining than sitting in the hospital waiting room. And mother continued supervising everything and everyone while she simultaneously tended to Daddy's moment-to-moment needs. I just sort of stood around all day feeling stupid with no clear idea about how I might be helpful.

To redeem myself, I offered to take the night shift and let Mother get some sleep. For now, Dad is resting quietly. I am alone in the room with the greenish glow and steady beep of the machines that track his vitals and reassure us all is well. I jump startled as they all suddenly start screaming at the same time, creating an ominous cacophony. Dad hasn't stirred, but I'm not sure that's necessarily a good sign. I stick my head out of his room and yell towards the nurse's station, "I think I need some help in here!" In a matter of seconds, nurses and doctors surround the bed in practiced response. I step back watching their choreographed efforts as directives fly back and forth around the room. I have no idea what is happening.

"Should I go get my mother?" I ask whoever happens to be standing closest to me. The doctor nods yes without diverting his attention away from Daddy who is just lying there. His eyes are closed and he's just lying there. Maybe I should have let one of my competent, older sisters take this shift after all...

I take off down the hall and go into the waiting room where Mom is stretched out on a cot sleeping. I hate to wake her, but don't dare not. "Oh, please, please let her end up being angry at me," I pray. "Let her be angry at me for waking her up for what ends up being no reason at all. " I rouse her with a shake.

"What's wrong?" she asks, startled.

"I don't know," I say. "But the machines are going crazy and there are a bunch of doctors and nurses in there and I thought you'd want to know."

She jumps up and runs towards his room with me at her heels. I follow her down the hall, but don't re-enter the room with her. There's nothing I can do to help. Better I stay out here. Out of the way. Nearby. After a while, things calm down. People stop rushing and voices lose their urgency and the machines return to their steady whir. I stop one of the doctors as he comes out.

"What happened in there?" I ask. He pauses, searching for a lay-man's explanation.

"You're Dad is having problems breathing," he says simply. He adds nothing to this Mother Goose explanation, but waits for me to wrap my mind around this obvious truth that apparently needed to be said. In the silence, we are both awkwardly aware of the steady rhythm of our easy breath.

"We're running out of options, aren't we?" I ask as I watch Mother through the doorway, tending to Dad at his bed.

"Yes, we are," he nods, "I'm sorry." I thank him and he walks away, going on to other patients, leaving me with our stark reality: this is one wild ball I don't know how to field. Not much opportunity for any magi-cal alchemy here. This is one bad throw that's going to be hard to turn into a great catch.

JAN
May 2000

Somehow I have found my way through six months without Hank. I still feel a deep penetrating sadness all around me and I still cry a lot, but not as much as before. Some nights I sleep well and others I don't. Some days I still feel frozen and in a fog, but other days I feel the spring thaw melting this solid block of grief. I am like a blind woman, feeling my way through to an unknown center–I am seeking my Hank-less core, hoping to feel hope and joy and peace again.

I didn't realize how big Hank was. His absence has left a huge hole in my life. I want to fill it with his touch, his love, his companionship, but it remains raw and gaping. I now realize every human being lives in a house with four rooms—physical, spiritual, mental, and emotional. I do not visit each room daily, but spend most my time in my emotional room as if it is a favorite parlor. At least I am opening the doors and windows. I hang a basket of flowers on my emotional and physical porch. I spend a lot of time on the screened porch, but haven't seen a single bird at any of the feeders. It seems when Hank left the birds did too. Even the crab apple tree and red bud seem to be mourning.

I say no to an invitation to travel to a friend's house and be pampered. I am learning what helps me and what doesn't. I have become an authority on my own personal grief. I am earning a degree in grief from the university of life experience. I do go to granddaughter Natali's college graduation; another celebration that Hank has missed. These moments continue unfolding without him, leaving me piecing together the past. I sort through family photos, copy pictures and put them in collage frames to give the girls on Father's Day—their first without him.

The emotional roller coaster I have been on for so long has mellowed into a gentle ferris wheel. Sometimes I'm up and sometimes I'm down. And from the heights of a good day, I gain perspective. The grief books I am reading tell me I need to list negative things about Hank and our relationship–they caution me against only remembering the good things and enshrining him. It is hard for me to do. I feel like I am backstabbing him, but I do come up with a few things:

1. He didn't want to travel as much as I did. Though he gladly spent money on things that would increase in value–our home, jewelry, antiques, etc.–he had trouble spending money on trips. We did go on a Caribbean cruise in 1990 and after he retired in 1995 we took a wonderful two-week trip to New England and went on another cruise with Babs and Bud. But we only had three years of playtime after he retired before cancer came calling. I wish we had played more, sooner. I wish he had seen the value of investing in experiences and memories.

2. He wasn't very social. Even though he would go out when invited, he preferred to stay home wearing old, comfortable clothes.

3. He wasn't open emotionally or even tuned into his emotions. When we were getting treatment in Florida, Lita and I were with him at the doctor's office one day and the nurse said we had been accepted into a research program to see if good sleep and delving into emotional issues would help reduce a cancer patient's pain levels. She handed us several sheets of questions for him to fill out and asked Hank if he'd had a happy life. He turned to Lita and me and asked us, "Have I had a happy life?" I was stunned! I told him that he was the only one who would know if he'd been happy or not! Good grief!

One day long ago he walked in while I was watching a television show where a psychologist was teaching a couple to sit eye to eye and talk about their feelings. He watched it with me and afterwards I asked him how he felt about something and he started to say, "I think…." I stopped him and said, "I didn't ask what you THINK about it—I asked how you FEEL about it." He got this serious look on his face and said, "I don't know the difference."

4. Sometimes he drank too much. He didn't go to bars after work. He didn't become abusive. He didn't spend money that should go to bills, but he drank quite a bit each evening after work, especially in the late 80s and 90s. The alcohol made him shut down more than usual. We talked about this several times and I was thrilled and relieved when he cut way back on alcohol.

But none of these things change my core truth. He was my armor; he positioned himself between me and the rest of the world like a shield. He was my comforter; he wrapped around me like a favorite blanket that kept me safe and warm. He was my partner; he shared my heart like a conjoined twin. No wonder I now feel hollow. No wonder I question whether I will ever again be blessed with the pulse of life force energy. It is only because I experienced his love so fully, that I now feel his absence so deeply.

June 2000

Once we experience the death of someone we love, we are so vulnerable to loss. Lita called crying, saying she is afraid I am going to die. A cousin called saying her mother is deteriorating quickly. Daddy called and said his friend Gwen has lung cancer; the prognosis is not good. Don says Jan is now in a wheelchair. A never-ending tragedy with revolving characters. All the memories since Hank's initial diagnosis wash over me, sweeping away the shaky foundation I have built for myself. I go to bed and cry.

HANK

(a letter written to Jan in April 1971 while she was hospitalized in Nashville awaiting surgery and he was home with Babs, Lita and Cammie)

Dear Jan,

I lay in bed at night with the scent of you. I remember your softness and your touch. The night is so long. It closes in and engulfs me with loneliness. I read, watch TV, listen to the radio, but the loneliness is still there. Even if forgotten for a second, something inevitably happens to remind me of you, a trivial thing like a piece of string on the floor which you would have picked up but now lays there still because you are not here.

Our lives have become so entwined that without you I am helpless and lost, unable to function properly because my whole being is filled with you. Perhaps the separation is good for me because when you are here I do not realize my need or experience the void, but whenever you are gone your absence presses down on me as if I'm in a nightmare where I cannot breathe.

After talking to you on the phone last night I was so lonely I thought I couldn't stand it. The darkness moved in and consumed my whole mind. I was very depressed and finally went to sleep late in the night.

I miss you.
I love you.
Hank

-

JAN
May 2000

My bed welcomes me like an old friend. I wrap myself in its waiting arms, turn on the ceiling fan, set my alarm clock for 9 a.m. and go to sleep. During the night I feel the bed shift as if Hank is getting in on the other side. I touch him and he feels cool and solid—just like he always did. We hold each other and I ask why he is here. He said he just came to see if I was doing okay. The alarm clock rings at 5 a.m., the time he always got up. I reach over to re-set it for 9 and notice the ceiling fan is off. Hank always turned the fan off when he came to bed. I am comforted by his visit. I get up ready to find my way through another day.

I go to Mayfield, Kentucky, our hometown, to visit friends and family. Old friends come to Indiana to visit me. Hank's mother has a birthday. I receive my notice of widow benefits from the Social Security Administration. Hank really is dead–even the social security office says so. And life really does go on without him.

I decide to start exercising. I paint my toenails for the first time in over two years. I start reading decorating magazines. I am emerging from a dark cocoon. I am transforming myself into someone who is not Hank's partner. If I'm entering the second phase of my life, I want to do so with some color and without this extra weight.

July 2000

It is the fourth of July and the sky is full. I look past the fireworks to the darkness beyond. The weekends are the hardest. I find that odd since we never did much on the weekends–I guess I just miss us being home together. As the girls grew up, Hank and I started dating again. Nearly every Friday night was our date night. We loved to go to a nice restaurant with a band playing where we could dance. I remember a long, straight, black, v-necked dress I bought on sale when Hank was ill. He loved it. He said, "When I get well we will go on a cruise and you can wear that dress and we'll dance." When we realized he wasn't getting better, he told me he was sad that he would never get to hold me dancing in that dress. One evening I went upstairs, put that dress on and came down to where he was sitting at the computer. I put my arms around him and he patted my leg, felt the satiny fabric and turned to look at me. His eyes lit up. He smiled, got up and held me. Though we could hardly move because of his breathing problems, we both enjoyed that last, slow dance.

I remember standing on the deck of a cruise ship on our 33rd anniversary after an evening of dinner and dancing. I gave Hank a card with a "poem" I had written.

THE ICE DANCE

I've always loved to watch skaters dancing on ice, especially couples. I've been thinking how a married couple, especially one that has been married a long time, reminds me of an ice dance…

There are times in the dance when the male assumes the lead and lifts and supports the female, at times raising her in the air, at times pulling her close to him as they glide in unison and harmony across the ice. As they continue following the learned steps, there are times when the female assumes the lead and with her eyes, hands and body weaves in and out across the ice, beckoning him to follow her. There are times in the dance when the couple pulls away from one another and does not touch; they are each doing their own dance. Completely separate from the other, they are each caught up in the rhythms of their body dancing to its own music. They come close together, then glide far apart–they are still on the ice together, just not in sync at that particular time.

When the Choreographer (God, or fate, or life) introduces new music that requires new steps, a change in the known, familiar patterns, it is at first difficult for the couple. But they communicate and practice, stumble and fall, get up and try again, all the time allowing themselves to feel the mood of the new music and teaching their bodies the new moves. Before long, they are again in sync, dressed in matching outfits, gliding with confidence together upon the ice, showing themselves and the world the beauty that comes from two as one in life's dance.

With whom will I dance my last slow dance? Hank won't be there to care for me when I get old. I realize I need to make preparations so I won't be a burden to my kids. I research long-term health insurance and go for a physical. My blood pressure is high and my heartbeat is irregular. (I am amazed my poor, broken heart is still beating at all!) I go to a cardiac clinic for tests. When I get there, I am overwhelmed by memories of Hank's illness. My tests are normal, but this white-coat anxiety causes my blood pressure to go up. I was never this way before; maybe as time passes my heart will learn to remain calm at the doctor's office, just as it is learning to beat on its own.

I am learning to fly solo in a world full of couples. I eat popcorn for supper. I continue to hunt for five things to be thankful for each day, but I have nothing to look forward to. Hank and I were always planning something. While he was ill, we were hoping for everything.

I still can't decide whether to sell the house. It was our home for 17 years and will be hard to give up, but I really think I need a smaller house with no steps. I refuse to remain in limbo indefinitely. I set a goal–by next spring I will decide. By next spring, I will have survived fall, the season of dying.

August 2000

My back is in spasms—they started coming intermittently after I lifted Hank's wheelchair so often. He has been dead for nine months.

The gestation period for my new life is proving to be much longer than a new baby. I get a letter from an old friend who is a Hospice nurse. She writes that it takes about 13 months for the average person's grief to begin to lift and feel more manageable. I am on a first-name basis with grief. We are very intimate with each other; it's hard to tell where I end and grief begins. I've learned to take Kleenex with me to the grocery; more than likely I will need it.

I go see the movie "The Perfect Storm" with Cammie and the kids. I watch half of it with my eyes partly closed. My stomach is in knots and I cry. I can't believe we spent money for such tension and sadness—I can experience that on my own for free!

CAMMIE
Memories 1999

The door closes behind me. Damn. I look at the coffee cup in my hand and smile again at the one million dollar bill printed on it. It gave me an early morning kick when I first pulled it out of the cupboard. It's Daddy's cup, but I've never seen it before—this cup has never lived in Indiana; it is clearly a Florida relic and I was going to return it to its rightful place in its Florida kitchen, but now I've locked myself out of their apartment. Well, I'll just have to take it home with me. It is 4 a.m. and there's no way I'm going to wake anyone up to return a coffee cup. Not even one with a million dollar bill.

Mom and Dad aren't even here; they're at Lita's house. The kids and I spent the night at their apartment and are now up waiting for the shuttle to give us a ride to the airport. We're returning home to Indiana after an unexpected, rushed trip to Florida. Daddy became worse and Mom called and we got on a plane; it was the first time I've ever purchased "grief fare." I cried because of the grief and because of the price of the ticket. It was outrageous, but we are way past caring about things as mundane as airfare. Thus, the irony of holding a $1 million cup–that is so typical of Daddy!

I arrived in Florida about a week ago when he started having bronchial spasms in his one remaining lung. He was transported back to Moffit Cancer Hospital by ambulance. They wanted to put him on a ventilator in intensive care, but he said no; he wanted to be with Mother and they wouldn't let her in ICU for extended periods of time. So they moved him into a large single room instead. If he wants to be with family, then family it is. Most of our out-of-state family flew in and we have spent the last several days together in his hospital room. What a roller coaster. He struggles and improves and declines and improves and struggles...it has been harrowing. And sweet.

Particularly the talk Daddy had with Jacob and Nick. With labored breath, he asked his grandsons to come into the room. He was sitting in a straight chair wearing an oxygen mask. They each knelt beside him so they could hear. "I'm not going to be around to help you become good men," he whispered slowly. "So I want to talk to you now." He told them: Do what you say you will do. Get an education so you can provide for your family. Save part of every paycheck. Pick up every penny you see on the ground. Spend money on things that will last.

The room was quiet and still. Then mother said, "Hank, tell them how to pick a wife." The silence deepened as they waited for Daddy to gather his thoughts. It was obvious he didn't want to give any rash answers here; this was important.

Finally, he said, "I don't know how to tell you to pick one, but once she's picked, she's picked. You treat her as if she would break. You are always faithful to her. You see that her needs are met. And when the children come along, you cherish them and love them and provide for them."

How many life lessons can be packed into a few days? We're all spent. Especially Daddy. Especially after last night. He was released from the hospital yesterday into the trusted arms of hospice. We all know what that means–he's dying. So instead of returning to their apartment, Mom and Dad decided to go to Lita's house; Daddy won't have to climb stairs and Lita can help with whatever happens next....

I sat with Daddy at the house all day yesterday while everyone ran errands and took care of business. I never knew illness came with so many details. Babs was helping Lita and Ken look for a house; they've been wanting to buy one and now seems like the time–since none of us are sure how strong or capable Daddy is going to be, they are look-ing for a house with an in-law suite that can accommodate Mom and Dad as needed. Other family members were out arranging for a hospi-tal bed and picking up nutritional drinks and I'm not even really sure what everyone has been doing, but I trust them to know more about what needs to be done than I do. I have been clueless for months.

I also know the family wasn't really expecting Daddy to be released yesterday. If pushed to the wall, I would have to claim responsibility for that although I won't readily admit it because no one seemed any too happy about it–I mean they ultimately wanted him to come home, they just didn't feel prepared for him to come home yesterday afternoon. But when I sat with Daddy the day before at the hospital, all I heard his weak voice say was that he wanted to go home. So I nagged at the doctors and nurses until they finally released him late in the afternoon. I think they were glad to have me out of their hair and the bronchial spasms had stopped for some unknown reason so he was breathing more easily and there really wasn't anything more they could do. Daddy and I haven't really talked about that part. Instead, I am celebrating the fact we made it home. Just because I don't admit to my family that I nagged Daddy's "unexpected" release doesn't mean I feel guilty about it...actually, I'm feeling kind of proud of myself.

"We did it Daddy!" I say after everyone's gone. "We got you home!"

"Hmmph," he answers.

I lean forward, resting my elbows on my thighs. His response does not catch me off guard; I have known Daddy to grunt or nod his way through entire conversations. "Are you glad to be home?" Maybe a question will coax some words out of him. He looks around at my sister's house. We are sitting in her living room with a full view of the open floor plan.

"Not home," his voice strains.

"Well, it's sort of home," I reason. "I mean, it's home right now."

His breath is shallow, his energy drained; he is attached to an oxygen tank and is waiting on a hospital bed and hospice services and nutritional drinks, but his focus is clear. He holds my eyes steady. "Home," he says weakly, "is Indiana."

Holy cow, he's talking about home, home. Like Indiana home. Like 24 hours by car and so many hundred miles it doesn't even matter how many–it's way too many. "Daddy, we can't get you to Indiana right now," I say. "This is home right now." He holds my gaze steady then looks around. His eyes come back and he raises an eyebrow. No grunt needed.

I suddenly realize my case is as weak as his voice. He's right. This isn't home in Indiana. Hell, it isn't even his apartment in Florida. It is a beloved family member's home. It is a comfortable residence where we feel welcome and loved. It's a nurturing environment that will be fully adapted to meet his needs and Mother's as well. But it's not home. Not by a long shot. Not by hundreds of miles.

Our eyes are still locked. He smiles then turns his attention to his index finger which has started "inching" across his thumb that is moving slowly, very slowly across his lap. We both watch this silent journey reach his opposite arm. I laugh as it starts the uphill climb to his shoulder.

"Daddy, what are you doing?"

He holds my eyes again and smiles. "Inchworm," he whispers.

"Inchworm?" I echo wonderingly. He nods.

"Inch home," he says. "Indiana."

Oh boy, he is serious. He seriously wants to make the trek back to Indiana. Slowly, inching along...how many hundreds of miles was that? Good grief. He holds my gaze as I lean back in my chair and sigh. His finger stops. He smiles, leans back in the recliner and goes to sleep, leaving me pondering.

I am still pondering and he is still sleeping when the family returns. I watch the house fill with activity. Things are brought in and put away. Storage is found. Phone calls are made. Food is prepared. Dishes are washed. Laundry is gathered. Furniture is moved. I watch my family make way for the next direction this cancer adventure is about to take us and all I can think is, "Stop. It doesn't matter. We're out of here, heading north."

All the hustle and bustle wakes Daddy. He and I watch the scene unfold around us. He smiles, looks at me and starts inching his finger over his thumb through the air. I sigh and stand up, hoping my added height lends me some courage. "Mom, can you come over here for a minute?" I ask. She heads our way talking over her shoulder to my sister about where to put something or the other.

"How are we doing?" she asks as she breezes over to Daddy and leans down to kiss his cheek. "Looks like you got a little nap," she says, looking at him more closely. "I'm glad you find that chair comfortable enough to sleep in." She unfolds and spreads the afghan out over him, then leans him forward to prop pillows. "The hospice nurse will be coming over later," she chatters. "I hope you're awake and feel up to talking to her while she's here. Although, you'll certainly have another chance. Someone will be coming at least once a day...." Daddy smiles at me and starts inching his finger again.

"Mom," I interrupt her. "Listen..." I pause, wondering what to say next. I suddenly realize that I don't have to relay the message that Daddy wants to go home to Indiana; he is obviously quite capable of doing that all by himself. He just needs me to help bring attention to the issue; in his weakened state, his voice is simply not loud enough to cut through all the activity going on around him. "I think Daddy has something he wants to talk to you about," I say.

Mother finally slows down. She looks at him and says, "Hank, what is it? Are you feeling okay?" That makes us all smile because that answer is certainly relative, considering his condition.

"Home," Daddy's voice squeaks. "I want to go home."

"What do you mean?" Mother asks.

"Indiana," he whispers.

Mother pulls back, but doesn't look away. "Hank, we can't get you to Indiana right now," she reasons. "It's just way too far to go by car and I can't imagine getting you on and off a plane."

She starts plumping pillows again. I nod. My mind has had several hours to run over this same path. I recognize each of these mental mile markers and I know the turn in thinking that waits ahead. In fact, I am so certain where this is headed, I decide to leave them to it and go fix myself some lunch.

Mother comes into the kitchen sometime later and announces to the room, "Your Dad wants to go home to Indiana." I keep chewing my sandwich as I listen to my family mull this over. I know where this conversation is going—Indiana; I'm just not sure how we're going to get there. We brainstorm together and quickly discard the possibility of flying or driving—neither seems plausible right now. Someone suggests an air or ground medical transport. We're concerned about the expense, but decide to research a carrier and get a quote. And that brings us right back to the here and now: a subdued group struggling with limited options and Daddy in the other room waiting on a miracle solution we all want to give him.

Mother speaks with clarity and authority, "In the meantime, we're staying right here." She walks over to Dad who has dozed in and out of the conversation. "Hank, we're going to work on getting you back to Indiana. And I need you to work on getting strong enough to travel." He smiles and nods, then goes back to sleep, apparently satisfied. The table breathes a collective sigh of relief.

Great, we have a goal, even if we don't yet have a clear plan. Better yet, he has a goal. He wants to go home. And I need to go home as well. Our grief-fare tickets are scheduled to fly out tomorrow and I don't even want to think about how much it might cost to change them. So I am completely stunned when my uncle suggests that I stay longer. As the afternoon drones on, his repeated request begins to take on a tone of insistence, hinging on desperation. He is visibly distraught, but I'm not sure what about. I mean other than the obvious turmoil swirling in our midst, what is going on?

"Uncle Bob, I need to go back to work," I stress. "And the kids need to go back to school. And Daddy seems to be stable enough. I don't see that there's anything else I can do. We needed to come, we needed to be here and I hope we were helpful, but it seems like it's time to go home. Is there a reason you think I should stay?"

"I just don't think your Dad has much time left," he answers.

I nod and cry. "I know," I say. "I know. But I can't just sit here and wait..."

"I just don't think it's going to be very long," he adds quietly.

"But we don't know how long!" I cry. "I can't just stay here and wait for him to...to die!" I am really crying hard now. My uncle rubs my back and walks away, not wanting to upset me more. I know he didn't mean to stir things up; I can tell he's expressing some genuine, heartfelt concern—I just can't quite figure out exactly what it is.

And neither can anyone else. Similar bizarre interactions between my uncle and other family members continue into the evening. Over a span of hours, my uncle appears to have taken on the weight of the world. You can see it in his posture and face. You can hear it in his voice.

Daddy has been moved out of the living room recliner and into a bedroom. A steady stream of hands and hearts wander in and out, checking on him if he's sleeping and visiting with him if he's awake. Now and then one of us will sit beside him for a while. Conversations range from tears to laughter as we all become familiar with this new rest stop in our cancer journey.

At some point there is no denying that it is time for the kids and I to go back to Mom and Dad's apartment. I am as painfully aware of our early flight as I am of Daddy's condition. I catch him awake and go into his room for a few quiet, final moments. "Daddy, I have to go," I explain. "The kids and I fly out early in the morning." He nods and I lean down to give him a hug. I am crying, struck with the realization that this may be the last time I see him alive. Knowing that, how can I possibly think that it's time to go? What last words do I say? Maybe my uncle is right; maybe I should figure out how to stay here indefinitely.

I no longer feel capable of making a sound decision about anything. I am completely spent, reduced to a sobbing, discombobulated mess. The best I can do is yield to whatever current comes by to sweep me away.

And that would be my mother. She comes in and sits by me and talks softly. I can't really make sense of anything she's saying, but Daddy must be listening. He takes my hand and says, "I love you. Now get going. Go live your life." Then he all but pushes me away with a strength I did not suspect he had.

Mother guides me out of the room, herds the kids, puts all three of us in the car and drives us over to their apartment. I am at best a zombie and may very well be dead because I can't seem to find my breath or make any sense out of the world that passes by the car window. The buildings and trees and street signs and people don't seem to come together to create any discernable images or cohesive storylines; nothing seems to have any relationship to anything else. It's as if everything is just floating around some great void. Disconnected. Just floating...

Mother parks the car, gets out, comes around, opens my door and pulls me out. The kids crawl out of the back and she ushers all of us up the stairs and through their front door. She sits me down on the couch.

"Now you listen to me," she says. "You need to go home. And you know you need to go home. I don't know what's going to happen and I don't know what got into your uncle tonight, but I do know you need to get on that plane tomorrow. So set your alarm. Go to bed. Get some sleep. Then get up in the morning and get to the airport. And call and let me know when you've made it back."

She stands there waiting until I nod, then pulls me to my feet, hugs me, pushes me towards the bedroom and walks out the door. Back to Daddy. Back where she belongs. At least she knows where she needs to be. With no clarity about what I should be doing, I obediently follow her advice and the kids and I finish packing and get ready for bed.

Not too much later, just long enough for 8-year-old India to put on her purple princess nightgown and start spontaneously mopping the kitchen floor on her hands and knees...(what is that about?!), the phone rings. I grab it in a panic, thinking the worst. It is Mom's voice, but she doesn't sound sad or scared, she sounds.....mad?

"Cammie, I'm just letting you know that I am coming over there to talk to you!" she says. Oh boy. Okay. I'm not about to argue with that tone. I review the day trying to figure out what I might have done. Nothing in particular comes to mind, but it must have been bad. Apparently I'll find out soon enough. A few minutes later she storms through her own front door. She definitely has my attention. I wait anxiously while she paces back and forth.

"Your Daddy!" she barks. "If I wasn't so worried about him, I'd kill him!" I stifle an emerging smile. We're going through an awful lot of hullabaloo trying to keep him alive just for Mother to end up killing him. At this point, if she really wants the man dead, there's probably some less violent ways to get the job done. I can't wait to hear the rest of this story....

"You know how Uncle Bob was acting strange all night?" I nod. "Well, that's because your daddy (it is interesting how her beloved husband of 40-some years has suddenly become MY daddy...) told him and your sister that he was going to die tonight! For heaven's sake! This afternoon he tells us he wants to go home to Indiana and then tonight he tells Babs and Bob he's going to die!"

"Wow," I say, unsure of an appropriate response. She's telling me Daddy says he's dying tonight but she doesn't seem to be in a distraught state of grief...she is MAD! "Why does he say he's going to die tonight?" I ask. "Did something happen?"

"Not that I know of, but that's what they told me he said!" she yells. "So I went in his room and asked him if he told them that and he said, 'Yeah' I did, but I've changed my mind.' And I said, 'Well it sure would have been nice if you had mentioned it to me!' I told him I'm the one who has been standing between him and death 24-7 all these months and the next time he decides he is going to die I better damn well be the one he tells! And it might have been nice if he had said something to you before you fly all the way back home!"

Wow (again). She has worked herself into a fury. The wrath of a woman scorned. Is apparently great. Even in the face of death. I guess I need some oxygen because I can't help but let out a yawn. Ooops. It gives her pause; her face and voice soften, "I just wanted you to know what all that commotion was about with your Uncle Bob," she says gently. "Your Dad told him and your sister he thought he was going to die tonight and asked them not to mention it. I just wanted you to know that's all settled now. I told your dad he wasn't dying tonight or tomorrow either for that matter. And I just wanted you to be able to return home knowing that. Now go back to sleep," she says. She reaches down gives me a hug and lets herself out.

Well, all righty then. Clarity at last. What a relief...

JAN
September 2000

A year ago Hank and I were fighting for his life. I remember asking him if he was sorry he'd had all the surgery and chemo and radiation. He told me no. He wasn't ready to give up; he wanted to go down fighting.

I have Hank's will on my mind and can't think what happened to it. I remember giving it to the lawyer and don't remember anything else about it. I got a letter from the bank about some sort of deed that I don't understand. It seems about the time I take care of one piece of business another pops up.

My insurance company refuses to pay for a doctor visit. I call them and they say my doctor isn't on my list. I tell them I don't have a list, but they argue I do. I call Hank's company and they say to call the insurance company back and tell them I have no list. I call back and talk to a different person who confirms I don't have a list, I have met my deductible, and my insurance should have paid the bill. I hate incompetence. "I'm a widow! I want to scream. "Be nice to me!"

I dread my upcoming birthday. I'm not only grieving for me, but also for all the things in this world that Hank loved that were taken from him. The temperatures are getting cooler. Hank loved the fall best of all the seasons. I grieve for his losses too.

I am dreaming about him more now. I don't always remember the dreams, but if I wake up after dreaming about him I want to go right back to sleep so I can dream about him more. The moon is huge, a bright yellow full moon. When I see the moon now I think of Hank somewhere up there. It is so hard for me to see a future.

Hank has been dead 10 months. I remember talking to someone shortly after he died whose husband had been dead 10 months. I remember wondering how she had survived that long. Now I am here at that place. You can either survive, try to heal, learn from this—or curl up in a ball, withdraw, become a bitter old woman. I refuse to do that. I owe Hank more than that. In two months it will be one year. I will have gone through the four seasons, all the special days that mark our lives. I will have done it alone–without my soul mate at my side.

I've gone back to things that have helped me in the past. I say the affirmation I used to say. I add a quote by Joseph Murphy: "I CHOOSE to put order in my thoughts and hang the walls of my mind with pictures of whatsoever things are of good report." I can choose to think positively or negatively. If I choose to dwell on positive things, I will feel better. I read in the grief books that grieving people will think they are better and then they will go through a difficult, sad time again. I remind myself this is a process! I have to give this grief time to work itself out. I still cry when I need to and read things that help me. I continue delving deep into myself.

All this sadness has worn down my immune system. I have been fighting sinus infections. I have finished several prescriptions and am still coughing. The doctor orders a chest X-ray. The X-ray shows an area of density in one of my lungs. I get the message on a Friday afternoon at 6 p.m. and have to wait through the whole weekend. I am scared of what they've found. I know sometimes family members of mesothelioma patients breathe asbestos fibers off of their loved ones clothes. There was an entire family in the hospital in Tampa; the father had been exposed at work and brought the fibers home. The mother had been exposed from doing his laundry and the daughter had been exposed because they had torn the father's work clothes up and used them as diapers. I'm not afraid of death, but after watching what Hank went through I am afraid of the dying process. And Hank is not here to be my advocate and caregiver.

It is a beautiful fall day. I go to India's soccer game with Cammie and Jacob. I tell Cammie about the message from the nurse and we both cry. Jacob hears us talking and wants to know what's wrong. I want to live for my family. I don't want them to have to go through another serious illness or death this soon.

A lot of people call to see if I have heard from the doctor. No news yet. Waiting is so hard. Waiting with fear is harder. I think I feel better now that I've started this last antibiotic. I think I feel a little stronger. I think I have more energy. I don't feel quite as tired, do I? Maybe I'm imagining it. Maybe I've become a hypochondriac!

Death makes the world unpredictable. It makes us all feel vulnerable. Grief is not a feeling in itself; it is a process that causes many feelings that share a common bond of fear. I fear that my pain has become an incurable disease. I open the windows and let in the fresh autumn air.

I remember a day last fall, before Hank died, when I sobbed all day long. Nothing he could say helped me–I didn't even know why I was crying. I was just tired and so very sad. He held me while I cried and cried. When people called, he told them I couldn't talk. Anticipatory grief can be as wrenching as grief itself. I will not anticipate anymore–I vow to live in the moment, unafraid.

The nurse does not call so the waiting goes on. Maybe I'll get better at waiting. I vow to accomplish something each day whether I feel like it or not. I revel in the power of choice. Finally, the nurse calls; I explain our concern about mesothelioma. She tells me to come in for another chest x-ray and a cat scan. The results show everything is fine. I walk out into the sunshine thanking God. I am so relieved! I dance to my car. I call and share the good news with friends and family. I am grateful to be alive. This medical scare causes an epiphany–Hank is dead, but I am alive. I don't feel well, but I am alive! This is a wake up call for me to live and enjoy my life for as long as I can.

Night has fallen. The doors and windows are open and I can hear the tiny insects. It's a pleasant evening. We are in the last days of summer, creeping up on the last weeks of Hank's dying time. I am flooded with memories of the bittersweet emotional palette of his passage. When we went to Florida for treatment, we thought we would only be gone a couple of weeks for the surgery and would then return home. We were so naïve! We thought we could continue any needed chemotherapy or other follow-up treatment back home in Indiana. But we quickly learned he needed to stay in Florida so the doctors there could administer the recommended protocol. We were in a motel room with tons of medicine, a wheel chair, oxygen tanks, and so many needs. We needed an apartment, furniture and our car that we had left at home.

A sweet couple that knew my daughter's family was going on vacation for a month in an RV and offered us their apartment, rent free, for the month. While we were staying there, an apartment in the same complex was scheduled to become available the day we were to leave the borrowed apartment. Then the traveling couple called and said they were in Indiana and would be happy to drive our car back to Florida. So many needs, each one met. If I only knew what I needed now.

The house and yard are beginning to look run down. I know I need to sell it and move into something smaller and more manageable, but my heart isn't ready. The key word to success in this new life seems to be manageability—I need every part of this new world to feel manageable. I give away all the firewood Hank had cut. It's much too heavy for me to handle.

A year ago, Hank was dying. His final death spiral started last October. The autumn leaves remind me. The cool autumn air reminds me. I can still see him sitting in his wheel chair in our foyer, looking out the front door, silently saying goodbye to his yard, the trees he had planted, the people and things he had loved. A year later, I stand here doing the same thing. I am silently saying goodbye.

HANK
(written November 1999,
four days before his death)

Dear Jan,

Babs and I are sitting on the front porch. I'm in my wheelchair and she is sitting by me in a lawn chair. I'm very tired and weak and don't feel like writing and have asked her to write my words to you as I say them…

I have learned a lot in the last 16 months. My love for you is much deeper and broader than I realized. Together we have faced an enemy, death, head on. I have fallen in love all over again. This time it is a deeper, more mature love that understands what is most important: to hold you close and just be with you.

I love you,
Hank

JAN
October 2000

Hank and I fell in love many times during our marriage and only had a few "divorce" periods. Those last couple of years we were so close mentally, physically, emotionally and spiritually. We were bonded in our fight against cancer; we faced head-on the possibility of our life together ending. We never loved any better than during those months— never cherished each other and our love any more.

How I wish he were still here, but I am learning better how to live without him. I realize I like myself. I have become my own good companion. I am easily entertained with books, needlework, writing, my home, family and friends. I no longer feel overwhelmed by deep loneliness. I have worked hard at healing and have earned the right to experience my loss in a new way. I have turned yet another corner in this labyrinth of grief. Of course, tomorrow I may feel as if I have crashed into a brick wall.

I drive to Lexington to visit Hank's brother and his wife. While there, I get a call from a good friend saying her grown son has died. I am not able to drive the five hours to the funeral; it is being held in the same funeral home where Hank was. I'm very fragile emotionally and physically and simply can't face that yet. How hard life can be. I hurt for them and the pain and grief they will go through.

This morning, for the first time since Hank's death, I woke with a feeling almost like joy. I do a little Christmas shopping. I meet friends for lunch. I buy gourds, make a fall basket and decorate the front porch for autumn. I feel myself unfolding towards my future like a plant growing towards the light.

Cammie is looking at houses and hopes to buy. I feel as if she and I are both on the verge of something exciting happening in our lives. Lita is working as a Hospice nurse and loving it. I am surprised she can do that kind of work so close to her daddy's death. I've invited all my girls and their families here for Christmas; it will probably be our last Christmas in this house. It looks like all of them will get to come. I'm looking forward to decorating.

November 2000

I flew home from South Carolina last night after a visit with my sister, Jennifer. I got off the plane at 9:30 p.m., got my bags, went out in the freezing weather, pulled my bags to the overflow parking lot and drove home alone. How far I have come in a year. I'm spreading my wings. I'm becoming more independent. I don't like it, but I'm doing it. I have often felt afraid, but I have pushed through the fear and that is real courage. It is okay to be fearful, but is good to push the fear aside and act anyway.

The kids come to help me rake leaves. So many leaves in this yard, each one a memory. A year ago we entered the last weekend of Hank's life. It was so hard on everyone. Many out-of-town family members came to visit. I remember Hank's best friend, Don, coming to visit. They sat together in the foyer, looking out at the fall trees, sharing very few words.

"Hank, what are we doing to do?" Don finally sighed.

Hank looked him dead in the eye and said, "I don't know what you're going to do, but I'm going to die."

After Don left that day, Hank asked me to help him die. We cried together and I called hospice and the girls and the family all gathered for one last weekend. Hank's doctor made a home visit and asked Hank what would help him most. Hank asked if he could get any relief from the fluid in his abdomen that was pressing on his one remaining lung making it difficult for him to breathe. The doctor said they could drain the fluid at the hospital so we called an ambulance to transport him. While we were waiting for it to arrive, Hank asked the girls to show the doctor our back screened porch and the woods and all the bird nests we've collected. They headed out back; I was glad they had something to distract them while the paramedics put Hank in the ambulance. The girls told me later that when they came back out front, the doctor spotted an abandoned bird's nest in a tree in the front yard and suggested they add it to our collection. He helped them get the ladder out of the garage and crawled right up after it; a simple act of compassion motivated by overwhelming helplessness. There was just so little any of us could do.

We all took comfort in giving Hank crushed ice during those last few weeks; it was all he really wanted to eat or drink. It seemed to satisfy and soothe him and he wanted a lot of it. But at midnight, the nurses at the hospital said he couldn't have anything else by mouth until after the procedure–not even ice. It was all I could do to walk in his room and tell him he couldn't have any more.

"They won't even let me have ice?" he asked. His voice was weak and defeated. It broke my heart. I told him if he didn't want to have the procedure we would go home and he could have all the ice he wanted. He thought about it for a while and decided that's what he wanted to do. I asked for the surgeon and explained we were going home. The nurse prepared a cooler of crushed ice to send with us. I crawled up in the back of the ambulance and calmly told the paramedics, "If he stops breathing on the way home, do not to try to bring him back." Hank nodded yes and the paramedics agreed. It needed to be said, but I knew he wasn't going to die in that ambulance; he was going to wait until he was home. I knew he wanted one last weekend.

I am so glad I was able to be Hank's advocate and caregiver during his illness and death. I'm so glad we were open with each other and could talk about his illness, his dying and what it would be like for me to be left behind. We both knew it was going to be hard, but knowing it in our head and me experiencing it in my life and heart are two different things. I've known people to tiptoe around death and try to comfort their loved one by saying things like, "You will be okay. You'll get well and go home," even if the patient wanted to talk about the reality that s/he was dying. I'm glad we had the courage to talk honestly from the very first day. I'm glad we were committed to being real.

Dear Hank,

I came in tonight, turned off the lights, lit the big candle and sat on the little footstool that holds so many memories of your illness and death. When you moved into the hospital bed, I moved this footstool next to it so I could sit here eye level with you while we talked. The night you died, Jacob moved this stool right up next to you and sat here holding your hand. Tonight, I sit here and look at your picture and all the mementos of our life I have gathered on this table and cry and talk to you.

A year ago yesterday, we buried you in Kentucky. A year ago today, we were driving back home. A year ago I was frozen. Like the trees I stood barren, stripped of my colorful leaves, facing the cold wind of life's new reality. It still doesn't feel quite normal. Since I was a child, I have worn the colorful attire of your love. I had a life partner and loved my role as lover and wife until the warm November night your spirit soared off without me. In the game of life we play the hand that we are dealt; my hand no longer holds my King of Hearts. I still love you and still feel married to you. But I can say I've made it through year one.

Love,
Jan

So begins year two of life without Hank. It's very warm outside and I have the windows open and love hearing the chimes. If Hank were here and well he would be out working on the woodpile. He would have on a "non-jogging" suit. (He called them that because he didn't jog.) He would have on a wool sock hat and his flannel plaid jacket he called a "jumper." How I wish I could look out back and see him out there working.

CAMMIE
Memory 1987

I pull up in Mom and Dad's driveway after a long day's work. Daddy is out in the front yard hacking away at the stump with his hand axe. The stump stands about three feet above the ground; its half-buried, half-exposed roots spread out about five feet in several different directions. It exhausts me just watching him.

"Daddy, why don't you just use some dynamite and blow that thing up or hire somebody to get rid of it?" I ask him.

He pauses in his work, leans on his axe handle and looks up at me. "Why would I want to do that?" he pants.

I take a good look at him, standing there bare-chested in his fisherman's hat, shorts and beat-up, untied, hard-leather, old-work-shoes-turned-yard shoes. Sweat is rolling down his red face. "Uh, because that's exhausting work and it's taking forever!" I say. "You've been whittling away at that stump for several years now!"

"And look at how much I've done!" he says proudly.

"But you're not even halfway through!" I point out. "It's going to take you forever to dig that thing out of the ground!"

"Oh, I see," he nods. "You think I'm doing this to get rid of the stump."

"Well, yeah," I say. "Isn't that the point?"

"Well," he says, "that's certainly the eventual goal, but it's not really the point. The point is it gives me something to work on, gives me some exercise, gives me something to do while I'm thinking."

"But Daddy, it's going to take forever to dig that entire stump out of the ground!"

"Well, not forever, but certainly a long time. But that time is going to pass anyway," he points out, thumping at the stump with the point of his shovel. "It will either be several years from now and I will have dug this stump out of the ground, or it will just be several years from now. We can't control time. We can only choose what we do with it." And he turns back to his work.

Over the next several summers I watch him patiently, persistently hack that stump out of the ground, roots and all. Not a remnant remains to stretch across the years as testimony to the children and dogs that now romp barefoot over that level span of grass.

HANK

(written while traveling February 28, 1973)

Jan,

   Be with me as I grow old.
   Lend me your strength.
   You are to me as the roots are to the trees.
   My strength emanates from your being.
I have matured with you by my side, patiently
molding me.
   Our seeds have been planted and are growing
into strong, sound plants.
   Soon we will be able to relax together in the
summer and fall of our lives.
   A time to laze in the sun,
   Absorb the beauty of our relationship
   And realize the unspoken dreams of our
youth.

I love you,
Hank

JAN
December 2000

The Christmas cactus is blooming again. Though I'd had it for several years, it bloomed for the first time last year, shortly after Hank's death. It had been in the room he died in; something about the experience caused it to blossom, like the new opportunities that now spread before me. They are both frightening and exciting. I don't know if I have the courage and the stamina to make major changes in my life. By spring, I hope to decide whether or not to sell the house. By spring, my wings will be stronger. I'll start with short, easy flights and then who knows.

Today's snow was perfect and lovely–big thick flakes that didn't stick to the streets. I was out Christmas shopping and it was as if I was moving through a snow globe that you shake to make the snow fall. I felt joyous and enjoyed browsing and finding treasures to give as gifts. I wrapped presents and listened to Christmas music. I went to dinner with friends. It is much easier to be with the couples, but Hank's absence still looms so large. They were all talking about their lives and the trips they will be taking. I looked and listened and was sad for me but glad for them. Now driving home alone after dark and coming in the house alone doesn't bother me. I allow my newfound courage to wrap around me like a blanket. I am no longer covered in a shroud. I no longer feel frozen or tied up in knots. I'm getting better. I am thawing, slowly clawing my way back to life.

CAMMIE
Memories

Legs wrap around legs, around hips, around waist, around arms that wind around head, around chest...hands grab, pull and squeeze. Daddy and I are on the floor playing a simple game with few rules, no props and no real objective. A fantasy game....I pretend I want to escape and he pretends he won't let me go. We wrap ourselves around each other in an endless array of constantly changing configurations until I finally "break free."

"What are you two doing?" Mom asks, hearing the commotion. She enters from the kitchen, towel in hand, the smell of dinner wafting behind her.

"We're playing knots!" I squeal and dive into Daddy for another round. He is spread out on the floor, smiling, waiting...we twist and squirm, grab, release, connect, burrow and squeeze. Happiness oozes out of me and trails across the floor, picking up speed until it takes flight, ricochets through the room and boomerangs back to wrap around my heart. The background hum of the TV spreads the evening news like a virus. But neither the Vietnam war, natural disasters or economic crises can permeate my childhood bubble. Daddy is home! All is right with the world.

We play a modified version of knots with just our hands and it actually has an objective: I try to get all his fingers down, curled tightly into a fist at the same time...a feat I never grow tired of yet never quite accomplish. Time and again, I methodically put each finger into its proper place one by one. But just as I go after the last one, another inevitably pops out. And as I corral that one, yet another one erupts. My developing brain keeps thinking it has something to do with the order I put them down, so I try sequence after sequence, an infinite variety of combinations, looking for the perfect pattern. This endless game keeps me happily occupied when the preacher drones on at church, or when I am fidgeting at a wedding or when my sisters' school play has gone way past that first mesmerizing moment of seeing them on stage.

Needless to say, by the time I finally figured out that his fingers would forever pop up regardless of the sequence they were put down, the game had completely lost its allure. And as a pre-teen, I finally became way too self-conscious to knot myself around Dad on the floor. But I was still hungry for the connection. So I started following him around the yard. He resurfaced the driveway, and I watched and talked. He worked in the flowerbeds and I talked and helped. He put up a fence in the back yard and I chattered away while he dug holes for one post after another. I talked about school. I talked about my friends. I talked about my dog. I talked about what I wanted to be when I grew up. I don't remember Dad saying too much; I think maybe I used so many words they sucked up all the space between us. But every once in a while he would throw out a choice phrase or two that would cause me to think myself into silence. "Always keep your options open" was one such gem. I pondered this particular pearl of wisdom while arguing with my sisters.

"Daddy said that somebody has to mow the yard before he gets home from work today," I announce. "He said that since there's three of us on summer vacation with nothing to do, there's no reason he should have to come home and mow the yard. He said he doesn't care who mows it, he just wants it done."

"Fine," they say flatly without looking my way. "Go mow it."

It is hot as blazes outside. The three of us are in the house trying to keep cool. One of my sisters is polishing her nails; she holds them eye level, scrutinizes her work, then shakes them around as she blows them dry. "I can't," she says. "I just painted my nails." I sigh and turn to my other sister who is doing her best to ignore the entire conversation, focusing instead on her own adolescent angst. She is beyond caring about risking the wrath of Dad's anger or the pain of his disapproval. She stares off into space and says nothing.

I consider holding my own in this battle of wills. I consider asserting myself in this endless struggle to challenge the status-quo imbalance of power between my older sisters and me. I will refuse to mow the yard! And then I think about the consequences. Daddy is not only going to be spitting mad, he is going to be disappointed. And then he'll either mow the yard himself, leaving my guilt to last much longer than it will take me to cut the grass in the first place. Or he'll launch a family "discussion" that will turn into an argument that might last for hours or even days. Or he won't say or do anything and will instead wait to see what happens. Which means I'll be having this same conversation with my sisters tomorrow and chances are one will still be painting her nails and the other will still be rolling her eyes.

I can suffer the heat or keep the peace. I am fairly certain I will have yet another opportunity to take a stand with my sisters, but maybe it would be wiser to choose an issue that doesn't violate a clear directive from Dad. More than likely, I will even have a chance to revisit this very same issue next week. Maybe by then my sisters will break their fingernails or be thwarted by a rash of maturity. Maybe Daddy will be so proud of how hard "we've" worked that he'll reward us with a grounds-keeper Maybe the city will come rezone our property line and we'll no longer have a yard to mow...besides, I have walked beside him step by step across this yard. We've sculpted this space together: a bit of shade, a burst of color, a touch of texture....together we smoothed the surface and paved the way. As much as I don't want to cut the grass, neither do I want to loosen this knot that ties us together.

So for now, I decide to keep my options open and my connection to Dad intact. I go mow the yard. But more importantly, I learn to make decisions from a perspective that helps me keep my cool through many future heated moments.

JAN
December 2000

I've spent several days working hard, decorating for Christmas and missing Hank. Each time I do something he used to do, I miss him more. He used to help me put up Christmas decorations. He liked it that I created a lovely home with a calm environment for him to come home to each day. He would look at the pretty decorations and say, "Don't we have pretty things?" and "You do such a good job of decorating the house." He enjoyed all the special foods I made.

He would go out and shovel the snow a little at a time. There is a ton of it out there now. It drifts into huge piles I struggle to shovel through. Patches of ice make walking treacherous and snowplows have pushed maddening piles of snow across the driveway. Schools are canceled and two to three more storms are forecasted this week. Carl offers to try to dig me out, but I tell him it is way too deep. I call the man with the plow on his truck and ask him to clear it. I want to be independent in my new identity as a widow. Since the onset of Hank's illness, I have humbly learned to graciously accept help that is offered and to ask for help when I need it. I am so grateful for the help I get from neighbors and friends, but I don't want to be needy. As I ponder my situation with this house, I think maybe I need a condo where outside work is done for me.

I think about the house Cammie just bought. I am so excited for them. She and the kids will be moving in January while she is still on break from school. They have a lot of work in front of them. Moving is such a big job. Thinking about it right now overwhelms me. She said she feels like something bad is going to happen. I told her every time we bought a house it was stressful and maybe that is what she is feeling. Lita is having some health problems. I hope it is nothing serious. It seems like something frightening is always looming. And the holiday season seems to have heightened all our anxiety. I don't want anyone I know to die this year.

It is terribly cold. I look out my window and see the dark silhouettes of the barren trees against the stark white mounds of snow. The earth has closed in upon itself. I miss Hank on snow days like this, when we would sit warm and cozy together. I miss dancing by candlelight and soft music. I miss cuddling with him, exchanging special gifts and saying and hearing, "I love you." I miss talking things over with him. I miss the companionship, the comfortable feeling of his presence whether we talked or not. I miss intimacy. My family and friends are wonderful, but I miss Hank.

But I have grown. I don't grieve deeply like I did. I'm doing things I've never done before. I'm gaining confidence. I'm not as fearful. This year I can listen to Christmas music without crying. Mostly, I'm at peace and content. I like to imagine Hank looking down and smiling when he sees me doing better or meeting a challenge with confidence. I like to think of his spirit near me helping me work through a problem. I'm amazed to realize that I am okay. I have learned a new dance.

THE NEW DANCE

I never quite liked the solo skaters as much as I liked the couple skaters. There seemed to be a special aura around the couple, male and female, moving together on the ice. I remember a few years ago there was a beautiful young couple with a small child. The husband and wife were excellent figure skaters and had won many awards and medals. He died suddenly and she was left alone with a shattered life, skating solo on 'new ice.'

That's how I feel now that Hank no longer "shares the ice with me." When he first got sick we knew our routine had been interrupted, but we had such hope that after surgery and treatments we would be "back on the ice, skating together again"–perhaps a little slower with fewer axles and tricky steps, but still skating together. But the Great Composer wrote new music and choreographed new steps—ones that I had to learn to dance to all by myself.

I liked dancing with Hank; our ice dance had become very comfortable. We worked well together. Our bodies moved in sync. We had learned the old steps well. But then he died and I found myself alone on the ice, aware of the cold air all around me as I had never been before. At first I just crawled off the ice, wrapped myself in a warm afghan, drank hot chocolate, curled up by the warm fire, and refused to even try this new dance. I could not have skated even if I had wanted to–the gallons of hot, salty tears I shed would have melted the ice around me—so I just stayed off the ice for many months. During those months I read many books on how other people had survived the deaths of their partners and learned to skate solo, or in some cases began training a new partner. I acquired a rather large library of these grief books. I also wrote down some of my thoughts. I gave myself time to heal before I ventured back on the ice, before I began learning to skate alone.

A few times I tried skating and would do quite well for a few days but then the steps would become too difficult and I would get off the ice and return to my comfort zone. The new routines were hard because for 45 years together, 42 of them married years, Hank had assumed the lead. With his strong body, wonderful mind, and gentle touch, he had made the steps easy. It was harder alone; if I fell, he wasn't there to help me up. If my muscles ached, he wasn't there to hold me when I cried.

But when we began our ice dance together, we weren't sure of how to do all the required steps–we had to learn to do the steps together just as I'm now having to learn to skate a new solo routine.

I will eventually get familiar with the new rhythms of my body dancing to its own music. Just like anything new, it seems strange and awkward at first, but the more I practice, the more natural it will become.

I have accepted that my composer, God, has introduced new music that requires new steps—a change in the known, familiar patterns. I began slowly to practice, stumble, fall, get up and try again, all the time listening to the new music and teaching my body the new moves. I don't like change; never have, never will. I was so happy sharing life's dance with Hank. We danced well together. I never wanted to skate solo, but here I am, back on the ice, not quite gliding with confidence, but not falling quite so often either.

I have a great group of supporters, friends and family who encourage me, clapping when I master a difficult step. And often, when I'm practicing this new routine, I see a dim figure way up in the stands, cheering me on and telling me how proud he is of me. I am certain that Hank is still my greatest fan.

I decide to entertain and have a couple of busy days getting ready for the dinner party. The house looks pretty and the table is beautiful. The food is good and the conversation is lively. I thank my guests for all they have done to help me during these past hard months. Carl prays and mentions Hank and I cry. It feels good to be a successful hostess. I wasn't sure I could ever do that again. Hank was always so much help when we entertained. I'm discovering I can do things I never thought I would do again.

My friend Don calls and tells me his wife Jan has died. He is going to have a rough year. I believe that men of my generation don't handle something like this as well as women do. If I had died first,

Hank would have struggled; I think it would have been harder for him to pick up the pieces of his life without me than it has been for me to learn to live without him. I go to Jan's calling hours and it is so sad. I dread the cold at the cemetery. I'm glad I didn't have to put Hank in the ground on a bitter, cold day.

The weather is so bad, I can't get to the funeral. I've thought about Don all day today. He isn't sure he can stay alone in his house right now. I think back to the first days, weeks, months after Hank's death when I was in such awful pain and didn't think I would ever have a happy day again. I wonder how I got from there to here. I have not only survived, I am actually enjoying life again. I no longer feel overwhelmed and hopeless; I feel fortunate and blessed to live in a wonderful world.

Then another death puts this family back on the roller coaster! On Christmas Eve, Cammie's ex-husband, James, is found dead in his home from a massive heart attack. It started out to be such a lovely week. Cammie, Jacob and India came and we went to dinner and a movie. We laughed a lot and had such a good time. Babs and Bud and Haley and Andy came for the holidays and everyone was in such a festive mood! It felt so good to be free of grief's brutal, oppressive hand. It's only been a year since Hank's death–this is too much heartache for such young hearts.

CAMMIE
Christmas Eve 2000

"He's dead," the voice on the phone says flatly.

"What?" I ask. "Who is this?"

"It's Roma," my stepdaughter says with exasperation. She repeats, "Dad is dead." Wait a minute, I think. What dad are we talking about here? My dad is already dead. Confused, I decide to temporarily skip the who part and move on.

"Where are you?" I ask.

"I'm standing in his apartment. The police are here. They're removing his body right now. The man is dead. It appears he had a heart attack and died in his sleep."

Suddenly it hits me. She's talking about her dad. My ex-husband. She's talking about James.

"Where are Amanda, Jacob and India?" I ask.

"They're in the car in the parking lot on the other side of the building," she cries. "They don't know yet. What should I do?"

"Drive everybody back over to my house," I say. "I'm on my way." I'm already moving towards the door.

"But, what do I say to them?" she asks.

"You don't have to say anything," I advise. "Just focus on driving everybody home safely. I'm on my way."

I am at Mom's visiting with her and Babs and Buddy. It is Christmas Eve and we are all gathering for what we expect to be our last Christmas in this house. Earlier in the day, my stepdaughters, Roma and Amanda, picked up Jacob and India and drove them back to Fort Wayne to spend Christmas Eve with their dad. When they arrived at his house, he didn't answer the door. They waited a while and then called me confused, wondering what to do. I suggested they go to my house and try calling him again from there. "I'm sure he just got tied up in Christmas traffic and will be home soon," I had reassured them.

When they called a little later saying he still wasn't answering the phone, I told them to stay put while I called the police. When the police said they'd drive over and check it out, I called the kids back and told them to wait at my house until they heard from me. I wasn't expecting this call from Roma. Wasn't expecting the kids would drive back over to their dad's house. Wasn't expecting them to find the police hauling his dead body out the door.

"James is dead," I say bluntly to Mom, Babs and Buddy as I hang up the phone. "I have to go." I have a single focus vision—to get to my children.

"Hold on," Bud says. "We'll drive you." We all jump into Mother's car. The 45-minute drive to Fort Wayne seems to take three hours. This makes no sense. We're just getting good at being divorced. It was only a little over a year ago that Daddy died. We've barely caught our breath. I can't believe this is happening. Not on Christmas Eve.

I walk into my house and find all the kids in the living room playing the game Aggravation. (As if we need any more aggravation!) "How's everybody doing?" I ask hesitantly, testing the waters. Roma gives me a pained expression from across the room and nods me into the kitchen.

"I couldn't tell them," she sobs. "I think Amanda knows and probably Jacob too, but I couldn't tell them."

Amanda walks into the kitchen crying. "He's dead, isn't he?"

"Yes, he is," I say simply. As hard at this question is, I'm glad it doesn't require a complicated response. I'm at a loss for words here.

Jacob comes into the kitchen. Same question, same answer. We all stand in the kitchen looking at each other. Then I realize they're all looking at me. Three kids down, one to go. India's still in the living room playing Aggravation alone. I go in and sit down next to her. She flashes a smile big enough to show her one dimple. But there is fear in her eyes. Her 9-year-old brain is busy between those blonde pigtails processing the confusion of the last few hours. But she doesn't dare ask the question her older siblings have asked. She fixes her grey eyes on me and waits.

"India," I say gently, searching for words. "Sweetie, your daddy is dead." She screams and throws herself in my arms, then pushes me away, knocking herself and the Aggravation game to the floor. So much for the mother-of-the-year award.

Now she's up again, pounding my chest, shaking her head, "No, no, no! I can't live without him!" (That makes the second worse news I've received today.)

"I know it feels that way," I say. I am fresh out of any brilliant words of comfort, so I shut up and hold her while we cry.

Good thing we drove Mother's car because mine wouldn't have been big enough to hold us all and I insist we all drive back to Huntington together. My mother-bear instinct is flared full force and I'm not letting a single one of these kids out of my sight. We all crowd into Mother's car, dog in tow. The trip must make him nervous because when we get to Mom's, he walks right in and pees on the fake snow that is laid out under one of the Christmas trees.

"Simba!" mother shames him. "I can't believe you did that!" He looks at her confused, as if to say, "Isn't that why that tree and the snow are in here?" Poor puppy. We're all confused. She rips out the soiled "snow," leaving a gaping hole in the middle of the decorated holiday fantasy.

When we wake up Christmas Day, I have no idea what to do. The Christmas presents are all under the tree wrapped and ready. But how can we just sit here and open presents knowing James is dead? On the other hand, if we don't open them, he's still going to be dead and the unopened presents will be a merciless reminder.

"Yes, we should share Christmas!" Mother says. "James would want it that way."

Not like I have any better idea. So we have coffee and Christmas morning casserole and open presents. We get caught up in the excitement of ordinary Christmas moments and forget. And then one of us remembers and tears spread through the room like a virus. Everything is surreal. By the time we're done, we have as much dirty tissue as we do torn Christmas paper. The holiday has definitely been soiled with a big, gaping hole.

JAN
December 2000

I call Lita and Ken who are flying in the next day for a holiday visit and tell them to bring funeral clothes. Other family members who weren't expecting to come over the holidays start flying in as well. We have certainly given the airlines a fair share of business over the last few years! We make the necessary phone calls and Babs and I sit up until 2 a.m. talking. I have trouble going to sleep; I can't stop crying. It's just too close to Hank's death and I hurt for these kids.

At the funeral, the four kids sit in the front row with James' family and we sit in the back. Cammie sits next to me, hunched over sobbing. She doesn't look up or speak. I can't imagine what she must be feeling. How awful this must be for them! It is just heart breaking.

Hank, age 14, when he met Jan

Jan, age 14 when she met Hank

Jan and Hank at Junior prom

Hank with Babs, Lita and Cammie

Jan and Hank on a cruise in 1990

Jan and Hank on a cruise in 1995

The tree where Hank carved his and Jan's initials
HAB (Henry Allison Ballard) --JHB (Janice Holman Ballard)
in March 1990

Cammie and James on their wedding day

Jan's 40th birthday with Hank, Cammie and James

Hank working hard to remove the large stump in our yard

Grandchildren--Nick, Jacob, Haley, India, Jessica, Natali and Sarah

Grandchildren--Roma and Amanda with Hank and Jan

Cammie playing the Taiko drum she built

Jan and Hank with Hank's brother, Bob, and his wife, Jenny

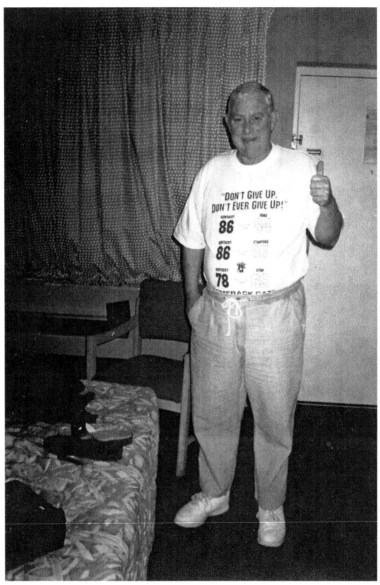

Hank the morning of cancer surgery giving a 'thumb's up' and
wearing a tee shirt that said, "Don't give up, don't ever give up"

Jan and Hank in Florida--Valentine's day, 1999--he is bald from chemo

The poster Babs made when Hank was very ill --with his 'motto' "Not convinced I can't fly" with all the family's hand prints drawn on it.

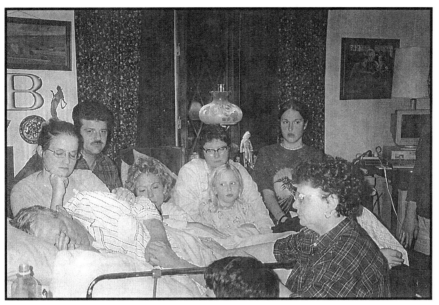

A few hours before Hank's death, November 8, 1999,
at home with family around him

Hank's tomb stone

Jan's 'meditation table' after Hank's death

PART II

"I can be changed by what happens to me,
but I refuse to be reduced by it."
–Maya Angelou

CAMMIE

December 2000

"What do you need?" she asks me. "How can I help you?" I close my eyes and try to organize my thoughts. It is the day after Christmas and I am on the phone talking to my best friend, Sally, about James' death.

"I don't know," I sigh. "I guess I need to get into his house. We need his clothes and eyeglasses for the funeral. And we need his driver's license so we can provide the morgue identification. And I just need to get in there and scope the place before the kids go in to get their things."

"Do you want me to go with you?" she asks.

"Well, the problem is, I don't have a key." I explain. "And I don't know his landlord's name or phone number. And the city's Office of Records is closed because of the holidays. So I don't really know what to do."

"Well, it sounds like we need to break in," she says matter of factly.

"What? How do you suggest we do that?" I ask.

"Come pick me up and we'll go over there together and figure it out," she reassures me.

I borrow my mother's car and drive back to Fort Wayne. "What is that?" I ask when Sally gets into the car with a small duffel bag.

"This? It's my breaking-and-entering kit," she says. "Didn't we decide to break into his house?"

My head is swimming. "You have a breaking-and-entering kit?" I ask incredulously. "Whatever for?"

"For situations just like this!" she points out. "You never know when you might need to break in somewhere!"

Good grief. I don't even want to know what a breaking-and-entering kit might contain. But she's right. I do need to get in James' rented house and I don't have a key. So I guess a breaking-and-entering kit is just what we need. And my best friend just happens to have one sitting right here with us in my mother's Lincoln Towne Car. My guardian angel appears to be on the clock after all.

We drive over to James' house and park. I sit in the car and take in the scene. His car is still parked in the unshoveled driveway blanketed by snow. There are no telltale signs of death. No flashing neon signs that say, "Tragedy struck here." In my mind's eye, I can see my four kids standing at his door knocking with snow-laced gloves, presents in hand, the excitement of Christmas wrapped around and between them like the cold. Surely they knocked several times. How long did they stand there before they disappointedly turned away and decided to go home?

I shake my head, clearing the picture as Sally and I get out of the car. She moves up and down the side of the house, scanning the windows. "I think this one will do," she says choosing the window closest to the back door. She pulls a tool out of the duffel bag and snips the screen then somehow pops the window open. I have no idea what just happened, but in a matter of minutes I am standing in front of an open window that bids me entrance.

"Since I did the breaking, you should probably do the entering," she says as she puts her tools away. Recognizing some logic in that, I step closer to the window.

"Give me a boost," I say and lift my foot. She bends over, laces her fingers together, cups my foot in both hands and hoists me up. Palms down on the windowsill, I heave myself forward. I am hanging half in and half out, with my tail sticking up in the air. "This is the last compromising position you will ever put me in!" I swear at James silently and then start laughing hysterically even though my stomach is pressing into the windowsill making it hard to breathe.

"Oh, for heaven's sake," Sally says. "Get in there before someone sees us and calls the police." She throws my legs inside. I tumble over a chair sitting under the window and onto the floor. "Now go open the door and let me in," she directs through the window.

I stand up and look around. The air is as still as–well, as still as death. I go open the back door and Sally comes inside. We stand silently together, listening to...dead silence. We walk through the kitchen and into the living room. Presents are lined up on the couch, waiting to be shared and opened. I grab the wall, steady myself and catch my breath. I am glad I am not here alone. And I am glad the kids are not here at all. They do not need to witness this post-death scene. The rumpled bed where his body was laying when they moved it out. The pre-made Christmas spaghetti sauce. The cheese ball platter. The unfinished work left on his desk. The journey through the house is a safari of surprises that jump out like wild animals clawing at my startled heart.

"Are you okay?" Sally asks as she puts her hand on my back.

"Yeah, I'm okay," I grumble. "Let's get what we need and get out of here."

We scurry around gathering his clothes, eyeglasses, wallet–all the essentials. Apparently, the initial needs of a corpse are similar to the needs of those of us who are still breathing. We close the window, grab her breaking-and-entering kit, and leave the scene. I am fairly certain I did not get whatever it is I am needing.

JAN
January 2001

There is so much sadness. Cammie goes back to work and school. I worry about her driving to Chicago in the bad weather. Jacob and India stay with me. We talk a lot and cry together. We have learned to do grief; we have learned grief is easier shared. I'm glad family was here over the holidays so we could support each other.

It is my first day alone since before Christmas. As soon as I wake, I get a shower, strip the beds and gather towels, bath mats, quilts, and blankets and throw everything in the wash. I am purging the experience of death from this house. I feel such a need to restore order. I take the decorations down, crying my way through. James' death brings Hank's death to the surface. I feel so sorry for Cammie and the kids and know I need to help her more. I can't imagine what it would be like to be a young mother totally alone or to grow up without a dad. What are all these deaths going to do to these kids? The ripple effect is just so far-reaching.

I miss Hank so much when a crises strikes. I treasured his wise counsel and was comforted by his support. I go with Cammie as she closes on her house. I take an 8 x10 framed photo of Hank so he is with us to share this milestone. The kids are getting excited about the move.

Now that James has died, I'll be going to Cammie's twice a week to stay with the kids while she treks to school in Chicago. I don't know how she keeps going. Things are going to be difficult for them for a long time. The grief and loss of James' death hangs over them so heavily. Cammie says India has been sleep walking out the front door. How scary. I wonder if it is stress from her daddy's death.

Cammie and the kids and I go to dinner. We see an elderly couple holding hands. "A year ago that would have made you cry," she says. She is right. I feel content, strong, capable, healthy, happy. It's hard to explain how I can miss Hank so much and still be content, I think I've just accepted where I am in life; I've learned to make the best of it.

Many people numb themselves with alcohol, pills, or exhaustion. If they don't give themselves the time and space and solitude to grieve deeply and thoroughly, then some part of the grief is not worked through and it festers beneath the surface like a wound that has scabbed over but holds infection underneath. I have not run from my grief, but have found the strength to stay still and let it hit me, wave after wave. I have embraced and welcomed the pain because I know the only way to serenity and happiness is to go through it. I have found the courage to let my heart crack open. I am so much better now 14 months after his death. I am a whole human being.

Diane tells me about her friend who was recently widowed. She said her friend was driving into the driveway at the end of a workday and thought, "This is how it will be from now on. I'll come home to an empty house." Diane asked me how to help her. I told her to tell her friend to take it one day at a time; to leave words like forever, never and the future out of her vocabulary for now.

I'm so grateful for my solid faith and for the people in my life. I am so blessed to have had a peaceful, loving, intimate, relationship with the love of my life for so long. Several months after Hank's death, I got a letter from a woman who had worked with him years ago. She wrote:

> You sound like you are making progress at dealing with loss. I have thought of you often. There are a very few couples I know who can make you think the institution of marriage is worthwhile. You and Hank were one of those magical unions or at least that is the way it seemed to us. You obviously enjoyed each other and were friends. I don't know whether that would make the loss easier or much harder.

As I reflect on my life with Hank, I remember how happy we were in Ohio. We lived in a new neighborhood where everyone was from somewhere else and we all needed friends. Babs and Lita married there and granddaughter Haley was 18 months old when we were transferred to Michigan. I didn't want to go, but Hank thought it would be good for his career so I went. It wasn't a good move. Cammie was thrown into a huge high school campus mid-term of her sophomore year. We moved in January and had snow up to our knees for months. I had trouble meeting people. Hank was sent to Florida to work a lot. And in May, my 58-year-old mother died suddenly in Kentucky. The years we spent in Michigan were three of the longest of my life, but I learned a lot. I grew up a lot. I learned to drive myself back to Ohio to visit my girls and their families. I learned to be more independent because Hank was gone so much. As I look back, I am so thankful for the lessons I learned during those three years because they sure have helped me since his death.

I go to Florida for two weeks for what has become my annual pilgrimage. I talk to Cammie on the phone; she is overtired and overwhelmed with packing and painting and moving and working and going to school in Chicago. I am sorry that I left her. She encouraged me to go, but I should have known how hard this move would be on her. Jacob is exhausted and India has spells of crying, and Cammie says she is really weepy herself. Grief is exhausting and she doesn't have the luxury of giving in to her grief; she can't give herself time to rest or sleep or write her feelings like I did. Even though she and James were divorced, they were good friends and co-parents. Now she is alone with the burden of providing for and caring for the kids. Life is full of such hard things. This is one winter all of us will be glad to see end.

CAMMIE
Winter 2001

Mornings are the hardest. During that first waking moment, it all rushes back; the truth washes over me as if I am hearing it for the first time. Daddy's dead. James is dead. Life makes no sense and I am the only thing between my kids and the chaos of the world...we are in big trouble for sure.

Nights aren't nearly as bad. When my day is finally done, I read, I write, I watch TV. I never lay in bed tossing and turning; I always keep myself focused on some task until I just collapse. Frequently enough I fall asleep exhausted on the couch with my eyeglasses and the lights still on, sometimes the remote control or a book still in my hand. But mornings are the hardest. That first moment of realization hits me anew every day upon waking.

On the days I go to Chicago, I wake at 4 a.m. I never set an alarm; I hate being jarred awake by an obnoxious blare. I just tell myself what time to wake up and some deep part pulls me from the depths. I look at my digital clock and it is always right on time. There is a wise woman inside me after all, but even she doesn't like the naked light of day. She rouses me awake and then leaves me to burrow my way out from under the shroud of warm blankets and re-enter my life.

On the days I go to Chicago, I leave the house at 4:30 in order to be at my 8:30 class. I step out into the early-morning night and robotically drive the two hours to the train station. I am always grateful for the extra two hours of sleep I catch on the train. But when I arrive at my train stop, I have to go through the process of waking up all over again. Good grief. By the time I get to class, I'm a mess. If I had known everyone was going to die, I would have never started this degree. I've considered quitting, but I am halfway through. If I quit now, I will lose the two years and $30,000 I have already invested. I am too far along to quit and too far from being finished to see any light at the end of this tunnel. I am stuck in the middle just trying to crawl my way out.

I get to class and we are doing a simulated movement group. My teacher puts on slow soothing music for the warm-up. My head circles and I wind down through my spine. My classmates and I move slowly through space, eyes half open, seamlessly changing levels from high to low, low to high. My movement quickly shifts from perimeter to core and I enter a deep movement meditation. Far away, I hear the music change. I know that the slow, soothing background has become loud and fast. I am aware that my classmates' movement has changed with it. They are now moving quickly, slashing and swinging and twirling and leaping through the room. But my movement doesn't change. I move with free flow, slowly, steadily, smoothly. I reach. I fold. I roll. Not off on the sidelines, removed, but right through the center of all this activity. I stand and turn and balance. I refuse to relinquish my core. I hold on to it in spite of the frenzy around me.

The group comes to a close and we sit together in a circle for processing. "Allison," my teacher says. "Tell me about your movement experience." I feel settled and calm, make eye contact, but say nothing. "Your ability to hold on to a still center in the midst of chaos will serve you well," she says.

Yes, it will. And it does. And my children too.

Daddy was always rock solid for me; he always provided me a solid foundation to lean on. It's the biggest gift he gave me. Though it seems silly in retrospect, I trusted he would provide that to my children too. But now he's gone. James is gone. Our pillars are dropping like flies. I want to be a rock for my children, a living, breathing solid foundation upon whom they can unwaveringly trust and depend. Not because I feel particularly capable, but because they need it. They deserve it. And there's no one else to do it. I may not be able to do it for myself, but the mother in me vows to do it for them. Paper, scissors, rock. The greatest of these is love.

JAN
February 2001

I look at the framed picture of Hank and me on the cruise in 1990. He looks so healthy and we look so happy. That was another lifetime. It was good, but it is gone. I am coping as best I can.

It is good to be in Florida with Lita's family and enjoy sunny weather. I go to a 50's musical at our local college and am flooded with memories. Music has such a powerful way of taking us back. Hank wore a white sport coat and a pink carnation to our Junior prom. When the young man sings about "a white sport coat and pink carnation" I cry quietly. It is my second Valentine's Day without Hank. His birthday is Sunday. He would have been 61. It's sad that we won't grow old together.

Dear Hank,

Your brother called on your birthday. How I wish you were here, healthy and happy. I would fix your favorite meal and give you a special gift. But you aren't here and I am! I'm doing pretty well. I still have bad days, but all in all I am coping. I'm sure this is a hard day for your mother.

I enjoyed being in Florida. I wish you could have seen the in-law suite finished. Lita and Ken and kids were good to me. You would be happy about Cammie's house. Babs is doing well in real estate school. I wish I could talk to you about selling the house.

You are still such a part of my life. We were one flesh and part of me is missing.

Happy Birthday.

Love, Jan

I fly back home to Indiana's winter weather. John calls saying he found the tree where Hank carved our initials: HAB + JHB 83. We walk down there together. I take pictures and try to get landmarks so I can bring Cammie and the kids. The bark is real crumbly and the tree is dying so I don't know how much longer it will stand. The foundation I have known continues to erode.

March 2001

March once again brings the hope of spring. I look out back and see the snow melting. Soon the daffodils that Hank planted will be blooming and the woods that he loved will be budding. Spring is coming and it seems like Hank should just come home.

It is Cammie's birthday. Jacob wrote the sweetest note on her birthday card. He mentioned Hank and James. She sobbed! I'm sure she feels alone. I'm alone also, but I'm coasting. Just me. No kids to raise. No job to keep. Cammie is in such a difficult phase. Oh, the passages of our lives. I am proud of the strong women our girls have become. And I am proud that there are now actually days and even weeks when I am happy. I am learning to like my new life.

Don comes over for coffee and we talk and share our experiences of being caregiver to our lost spouses. I tell Don I loved Hank with everything in me and cared for him the best I could and would have done anything for him. I am sure he did the same. I am proud of us for caring for our loved ones in our homes.

I continue to get rid of stuff and clean closets. I got the box down off the closet shelf and read all the cards Hank has given me through the years. One touched me in a special way—it was about us growing old together. Mesothelioma prevented that from happening.

Now that it is spring, it is time to make a decision about the house. I've made a plan and discuss it with friends John and Diane. I will:

- Continue getting rid of clutter and straightening closets
- Get an estimate on an asking price for this house
- Begin looking at homes, condos etc to see what is available
- Put it on the market after I've found something I'm interested in
- Continue to pray about it and sleep on it
- Trust my feelings

I know once the house is sold, I can't get it back so I have to make sure and make the right decision. If it's supposed to sell, it will sell. If not, it won't. I'm trying to push the fear of the unknown aside and plunge ahead. It's the scariest thing I have ever done on my own. Always before it was us, party of two, making the decisions and discussing pros and cons of everything that came up. Now it is just me. Am I ready to be out there on my own? Am I grown up yet?

I realize I have been sitting here with clenched fists, desperately trying to hold on to the past. I am trying to walk a fine line of keeping Hank and all we shared in my heart and mind while embracing life and moving on. Today, I physically lift my open palms to the sky, symbolically releasing my old life and reaching toward the new life that's waiting for me–whatever that might be. Change is part of that–whether it's changing a home or a room, I am moving out of my comfort zone. I have reached a milestone, a turning point in this process. I am learning to push fear aside and do things. I am practicing the new steps to a new dance.

I'm so thankful I've come so far in my grief journey. I think Hank would be proud of me. I remember the conversation we had the day before he died. He was so weak, he could barely whisper. He told me just because he was dying, he didn't want me to die too. He held me and we cried together. I am still walking and talking and breathing. I am embracing life and I am okay!

CAMMIE
Memory 1985

"What are your plans after you graduate college?" Dad's best friend Don asks me.

"Do you want to hear my short-term or long-term plans?" I query back. Don and I are sitting on the deck talking while we wait for dinner to finish grilling.

Dad walks through the sliding glass doors and Don gives him a look that causes him to pause. "What?" he asks, glancing back and forth between us. "What's going on?"

"I'm asking your daughter about her plans after college," Don explains.

"Oh that," Dad says. "I used to worry about how to motivate her. Now I have problems keeping up with her."

It is the summer of my junior year of college. After a dismal high school experience, I have redeemed myself. High school teachers used to tell me it was a shame my intelligence and creativity were wasted by my laziness and cocky attitude. I now have a double major in magazine journalism and political science with a cumulative GPA to be envied and an emerging portfolio that speaks highly of my potential. I have been accepted into an international student exchange program and have arranged to spend my senior year at the Chinese University of Hong Kong. I want to be a foreign correspondent specializing in United States/Chinese relations. I have staked a claim to my future.

"Do you plan to stay in Asia after you graduate?" Don asks. Mother cringes and looks away while Dad waits for my answer.

"I don't know," I say honestly. "I guess I'll just have to see how things work out."

"One thing's for sure," Dad says. "If you want to be a writer, you need something to write about." Don nods.

"Well I don't know why you have to go to Hong Kong," Mother says.

"Why can't you just write about things right here at home?" She goes back into the kitchen.

I am excited about going overseas and studying abroad until I am waiting to board the plane. I suddenly can't remember one single reason why I want to finish school in Hong Kong. "Why am I doing this again?" I ask Mom and Dad as we sit in the Chicago airport.

"Beats me," Mother says. "I have never understood why you are doing this. I never did think this was a good idea."

Dad looks out from behind his newspaper and pauses before answering. "Because you are ready," he says reassuringly. "You'll be all right. You're just scared." He returns to his paper that serves as a screen between us. I am unable to read his face and doubt he wants to read mine.

Hell yes I'm scared. Hong Kong is halfway around the world, more or less. I suddenly realize that if you're going in a circle, halfway around is as far as you can go before you start heading back. I am going about as far away as is physically possible. If I went any farther, I'd be heading back home. I feel a little panicked and wonder if it is too late to change my mind. I wonder if I can go ahead and cash in that open-ended, round-trip, just-in-case ticket. They announce my plane is boarding.

"Here we go," Dad says as he stands up. I sit there stupidly as if I am in a mild state of shock and don't know what to do next. He reaches for my hand and pulls me to my feet. He grabs my bag and hands it to me. He turns me towards the woman who is taking boarding passes. "You're going this way," he says and nudges me forward. Mother and I are crying and holding on to each other. Dad pries us apart, gives me a hug, clears his throat and steps away. Suddenly, I am walking down the boarding ramp. I am moving through a portal that is thrusting me towards an unknown future. I stop and look back. Mother waves; she is still crying. Dad nods and smiles.

At some point during the long flight, my excitement grows stronger than my fear. I discover that after traveling for 24 hours, one can be completely disoriented to time, people and place when one arrives. At the airport, I figure out how to exchange money and "queu" for a taxi. I don't end up having to tell the taxi driver or the dispatcher that I want to go to the Chinese University of Hong Kong. Instead, unable to break though the language barrier, the poor taxi driver takes me all over Hong Kong, obviously hoping at some point he will randomly drive by my destination. He and I are both relieved when I finally see the university's sign and say, "Stop!"

While a student in Hong Kong, I study Mandarin Chinese and immerse myself in the culture. I fall in love with a Chinese man, Henrie, and am surprised by a positive pregnancy test in December. Determined to graduate on time, I only share this information with Henrie. I do not tell Mom or Dad until spring.

"Hey Daddy, how are you?" I say into the phone, still amazed I can talk to people on the other side of the world.

"Good, how are you?" he answers, surprised to hear my voice. "What are you doing calling us?" he asks good-naturedly. Though Mom and I write often enough, we have all agreed to only talk on the phone on holidays and special occasions; otherwise, our phone bill would be outrageous. He doesn't yet recognize this phone call as the special occasion it is; certainly one that will be forever etched into all our memories.

"Well, I have something to tell you," I say into the hard, cold receiver. "Is Mom there?"

"Yes, she's right here. What's up?"

"Well, I don't really know how to say this, but I'm kind of pregnant."

"How can you be kind of pregnant?" he asks. "You either are or you aren't. How pregnant are you?"

"About five months," I explain.

"Here, talk to your mother," he says and hands her the phone.

"Cammie, what's wrong?" Mom asks worriedly.

"Well, nothing's wrong exactly," I stall for time. "I'm fine. Pregnant, but fine. About five months pregnant actually. I just haven't really known how to tell the two of you, but I realize I have to tell you sooner or later," I ramble. "I mean, you're going to notice when I come home in May for graduation and even if I don't come home in May, the baby is due in August so you're definitely going to know eventually." More rambling. "So I decided to just go ahead and call and tell you, but now I'm not sure that was such a good idea. Maybe I should have just waited till I was home and let you figure it out yourself....Mom? Mom, are you there?"

Suddenly Daddy's back on the phone. "You need to use that return trip ticket and come home," he says.

"Daddy, no!" I insist. "I need to finish this last year of school. I mean especially now. The baby is due in August. It will be too hard to finish school next year after it's born. I'm fine, really I am, and I want to be here with Henrie. I need to stay here right now, but I want to come home in May for graduation like we planned. I want to see both of you and then I'll come back and have the baby here. But we have time to talk about all that later." Silence on the line. "Hello? Dad, are you there?"

They are obviously playing roulette with the phone because Mother's voice is back again asking, "Are you getting married? This is just all such a shock!"

I don't know how much of the earlier conversation she has heard and am not sure she'll stay on the line long enough to make it worth repeating. "I know Mom, I know. Look, everything is okay," I reassure her. "I'm fine and Henrie and I love each other and no, I'm not getting married right now, but I'll be home in May and we can talk about all this then, okay?" So much for being a professional communicator.

I do go home in May and I do graduate. I expect to return to Hong Kong to have the baby and start my life, but my visa is denied because I am too far along in my pregnancy. I must stay home through the summer and have the baby in the States. Mom and Dad generously and graciously offer me refuge.

As my belly grows bigger, I am grateful to be in safe, familiar sur-roundings. I am grateful to have the opportunity to share this experience with my mother. I no longer talk about adventurous plans. Instead, we talk about nursing and teething and Henrie. Henrie and I write fre-quently and talk on the phone occasionally. I look forward to everyone meeting each other. With Henrie's blessing, I plan a wedding to take place the following summer at Mom and Dad's house; Daddy offers to buy Henrie a ticket so he can be at the baby's birth. Henrie says his work schedule will not allow such travel, so we resign ourselves to re-uniting in Hong Kong after the baby is born.

After our sweet, beautiful, baby Jacob is born. Heart of my heart and soul of my soul—has he not always been a part of me? Was there ever a time when my entire world did not evolve around when he eats and sleeps and smiles? I can't travel with him until we have a birth cer-tificate. And a social security card. Then a passport. And a visa. While we wait for paperwork to be processed, Mom and Dad and I celebrate when Jacob rolls over and sits up and starts using his hands and sud-denly he is six months old and I am once again getting on a plane but this time I am taking Jacob with me. This time we are all crying as I carry this baby boy we have all grown to love down the boarding ramp towards an unknown future.

I see this future very differently through the eyes of a mother. I am living at Henrie's house with his family. Suddenly, it is very important to me whether or not the window is open or closed, what time we all wake up and go to bed, whether or not the dishes are washed in hot water or cold. Suddenly, it bothers me that I don't understand the conversations Henrie has with his mother–I can tell they are talking about Jacob, this first-born son of a first-born son. I can tell they are discussing him and making decisions about him, but I am left out of the jet-lagged loop. I have only been back in Hong Kong for a couple of days, but I realize I don't want to raise my son in this faraway land with strangers.

So I start talking to Henrie about the life we will build together when we go the States next summer to be married. He answers me with a strange, awkward silence that creates a chasm between us I have no idea how to bridge. I am disoriented and exhausted, but my mother instinct is far from subdued; my antennae is vigilantly alert as I watch Henrie and his mother take over the care of Jacob and I consider what to do.

On day three, I call Mom and Dad as planned. I try to describe what I imagine would be a normal adjustment. I don't want to tell them that Henrie has told me he has no intention of going to the States next year to be married. That indeed he can't even get out of Hong Kong because he owes the equivalent of several hundred thousand US dollars in back taxes and that he didn't tell me because, as a woman, the family finances are none of my business.

I try to sound light and happy and confident, but they know me too well.

"What's wrong?" they ask. We talk our way through, exploring different options.

"Daddy, I just don't know what to do!" I lament.

He pauses, then speaks with decisive clarity. "I'll tell you what to do. You get that baby and get your ass on the next plane home!" Another pause and then he adds, "You can decide the rest from here. You'll be able to make better decisions from a place of safety."

Good decisions from a place of safety. That makes sense AND it feels good. Suddenly I see a yellow brick road stretching out before me and it leads to home.

"Get that baby and get your ass on the next plane home!" His words ring in my ears. Time to cash in that open-ended, round-trip, just-in-case ticket.

I call the airlines and find out I can be on a plane in two hours or two weeks; everything else is booked because of Chinese New Year. I call the Consulate General, Eugene, who was my previous professor and ask him for help. I wait for Henrie to leave the house and then wake Jacob from his nap much to Henrie's mother's dismay. I ignore her disapproving gestures and undecipherable verbals and carry my sleeping son down eight flights of stairs and into a cab. I take him to Eugene's house and let him babysit while I go retrieve my plane ticket, passport and cash from the bank's safe deposit box. My adrenaline is pumping full force. When I think I must surely be losing my mind and should slow down, take a deep breath and reconsider such a drastic step, I hear Dad's voice saying, "Get your ass on a plane!" So I robotically continue following that directive.

I call Henrie on the phone. "I am coming to get my things," I tell him. "I am boarding a plane in an hour and taking Jacob with me. I am going home." No discussion, just the bare, hard facts. He is yelling, asking me where Jacob is. I hang up the phone.

Eugene sends a Marine with me back to Henrie's house. The Marine sits calmly watching the showdown from the couch. Henrie and I are yelling at each other. His mother is sprawled on the floor, belly down, holding onto my ankle for dear life; I drag her through the apartment as I gather my things and throw them into the suitcase that is open on the bed. I drag her with every step as I gather more things and return to the bed, only to find his sister is taking things out of the suitcase as fast as I am putting them in. I finally sit down, ready to give up in exasperation.

"Surely this isn't necessary," I think to myself.

"Get your ass on the next plane home!" I hear Daddy say.

The plane that leaves in an hour, I remind myself.

So I throw everything within reach into the suitcase and zip it up. I pry the clasped fingers off my ankle, nod at the Marine and we escape for the door.

"You can come to the airport to say goodbye to Jacob if you'd like," I say to Henrie and he follows me out. We travel in a cab and go up to Eugene's apartment together to pick up Jacob. Eugene secures Jacob in a carrier that is tied around my torso so he sits at my chest.

"Do not take this baby out until you are sitting on the plane!" he warns me while he gives Henrie a deadpan stare. Baby secure, Henrie and I travel to the airport alone, together, crying. Henrie begs me to reconsider, which I consider doing until Dad's voice breaks through yet again. "Get your ass on a plane!"

His voice propels me down yet another boarding ramp, through another portal to an unknown future where I will be able to make good decisions from a place of safety. Jacob and I are returning home to the heartland.

JAN
April 2001

I have been putting off working in Hank's study. That room is difficult for me. But yesterday I worked in there for hours. He has been gone 17 months and I am just now able to go through his files and see his handwriting and all his neat little rows of numbers without falling apart. I read each piece of paper and put it in a pile to be kept, shredded or thrown away. It is taking a long time, but I am doing it. I'm moving in the right direction. I bring down all my tax papers, organize them and put them in Hank's brief case to take to the CPA next month. I can't bear to part with his briefcase. I gave it to him a few years ago for an anniversary gift; he was so proud of it and used it every day.

I am sad today as I get rid of some more of Hank's things. I seem to be getting rid of more and more of him. A few months ago I still needed some of his things, but now I can let more of them go. A few weeks ago I gave some of Hank's and my rings to Babs, Lita and Cammie. My left hand is now bare, which seems strange. I've had that gold band on my left ring finger for a long time. I stopped wearing his watch today and will get a new battery for mine.

Dear Hank,

I wish you could have been here today well and healthy. You would have enjoyed the day so much. Friends John and Nancy came to visit from North Carolina. All our local friends were here as well and the men played golf. John used your clubs and said they were great. I gave him your books on management and quality control. I think you would have liked for him to have them. I'm giving more and more of you away. All the guys were giving me advice on selling the house and buying one.

Honey, I miss you so but I am making progress. I am still trying to be positive and count my blessings. I looked at the full moon tonight and thought of you. I heard 50's music in a store and wanted to dance with you. Will I ever dance again?

Love,
Jan

Today is Daddy's 82nd birthday. His mind is good but his body is failing. We are all getting older except Hank. He is forever 59.

The realtor came today and told me what she thinks I can get out of the house. The next step is to look around and see what I like and can afford. I'm scared and excited. I am constantly thinking, "This may be my last Easter in this house. This may be the last time I do the paths out back, or the flowers out front, or the last year Jacob mows." I feel a little panicked thinking of all the physical work I will have to do if the house does sell. I am learning how to get things done without a partner. I hire people to help as needed.

The realtor and I have looked at ten houses. Some were nice, but each had something I didn't like. I look out at my lovely wooded back yard and my nice shady screened porch and feel very confused. Being part of a couple is so wonderful because your joys are doubled and your problems are halved when you share them with another. Now I'm just confused. Alone and confused. Cammie and the kids and I meet the realtor at one house that I like. The back yard has a privacy fence that hides the nearby train track. We can't see the train that rumbles by as we pull up, but we can sure hear it.

"There is no way I could buy a house with a train in the back yard!" I tell Cammie.

We go inside and look. It has spacious rooms. A nice floor plan. A lot of light. Divider walls that circle the room with shelves. I tell the realtor to make an offer.

"Mom, you just said you couldn't buy a house that close to a train!" Cammie says.

"Well, if other people have gotten used to it I can too," I claim.

We leave and I burst into tears. " I don't know what's wrong with me," I cry. "I can't live in a house with a train that close!" I am all over the place emotionally and have been having night sweats and hot flashes. I have asked God and Hank to guide me through this, but they aren't helping.

"Mother, why don't you call the realtor and tell her not to make an offer," Cammie suggests. "And maybe you need to not look at any more houses for awhile." She reminds me that my deadline to make a decision by May 1 is self-imposed and there is no reason I have to make a decision by that day. I breathe a sigh of relief and make the call. I seem to be a little insane right now.

Babs calls and I tell her all about the train house. "Well, God is watching out for you," she says. "He had the train go by while you were there so you would hear it." Good point. I make an appointment with the doctor to see if all these physical and emotional symptoms could be related to the estrogen he took away.

I go to the hardware store and tell the man I am a widow whose tub needs caulking and I need help. He shows me what to buy and tells me how to do it. I go home and work on the tub. Maybe I am just supposed to stay right here in this house.

Now that I'm not looking at houses, I have more time to work in Hank's study. I have gone through almost all his files. It's still emotionally draining; his study was his place. He loved sitting at his desk taking care of our financial business. And I loved it too.

I take Daddy to dinner and tell him he is my Saturday-night date. "If a nice young man comes along, go out with him," he says. "Life is too short to be lonely." For someone who rarely talks about anything personal, he cut right to the chase. I drop him off and sob all the way home.

I am weepy all week. I talk to Hank's picture and cry. I make the mistake of watching the movie "Ghost." I hadn't seen it in a long time and thought it might be comforting. I was wrong. I sob and scream at Hank and God. I haven't been like this in a long time. I thought I was making progress, but now I feel I have slid all the way down the hill of grief and have to climb it all over again.

I go to an open house of model homes in a lovely wooded neighborhood in town. I can afford one particular house plan on one particular lot. I go home lonely. I turn to my refrigerator for some inspiration and read the words I have posted there:

- "Courage is the power to let go of the familiar," by Raymond Lindquist.
- "If we don't change, we don't grow, if we don't grow we aren't really living," by Anatole France.
- "Change is the only evidence of life," by Evelyn Waugh.
- "Getting over a painful experience is much like crossing monkey bars. You have to let go at some point in order to move forward." (Author Unknown)
- "Moving on is a simple thing, what it leaves behind is hard," by Dave Mustaine.
- "Everyday courage has few witnesses. But yours is no less noble because no drum beats for you and no crowds shout your name," by Robert Louis Stevenson.
- "The journey between what you once were and who you are becoming is where the dance of life really takes place," by Barbara Deangelis.
- "Let your mind start a journey through a strange new world. Leave all thoughts of the world you knew before. Let your soul take you where you long to be. Close your eyes, let your spirit start to soar and you'll live as you've never lived before," by Erich Fromm.

- "It is good to have an end to journey towards, but it is the journey that matters in the end," by Ursula Leguin.
- "Heroes take journeys, confront dragons and discover the nature of their true selves," by Carol Pearson.
- "The only journey is the journey within," by Rainer Maria Rilke.

In the midst of all this change, I try to imagine what a normal week would be like. It seems as if I haven't had a normal week since Hank got sick over two years ago. I am trying to create a new normal, but it keeps getting interrupted–by James' death, by me traipsing back and forth to Fort Wayne each week to look at houses and to help Cammie with the kids. There is no normal. It will soon be India's birthday and neither James nor Hank are here to see her grow up or see any of the kids marry or build careers or have children. No little girl should have to grow up without her daddy and her granddaddy. Where is the normalcy in that?

CAMMIE
Memory 1988

I cannot believe it. Two-year-old Jacob has chewed his peanut butter and jelly sandwich into the shape of a gun and is now shooting its limp barrel across the table. How absolutely, unbelievably creative of him. I have vowed he will not have toy guns. The idea of teaching my young son to wield a weapon makes my skin crawl. The image of him actually holding a gun–even a toy gun–makes me more than a little dizzy. So I have laid down the law. No toy guns. He is now making guns. Out of everything.

The other day he asked Mother for tape. When my curiosity followed him into the living room, I found him taping his blocks together into the shape of a gun.

"Bang! Bang!" he said, as he pulled his hands up to his face and looked down the "barrel." With muscle control that was developmentally unnatural, he closed one eye, squinted the other and puckered his lips to make a whooshing sound. How does he know how to do that? He didn't seem to be doing it defiantly. There didn't seem to be any anger. He seemed to be happily filling his natural heart's desire—to shoot. I'm not sure if I should feel disturbed or proud.

"Jacob, put your sandwich down," I say. "Your sandwich is not a gun. You need to eat it, not shoot it." He scowls at me from across the table and puts it down.

"We don't shoot guns at the table, Jake," Dad says.

"We don't shoot guns at all!" I clarify.

"Why?" Jacob asks. His favorite question these days. Dad pauses eating and looks at me, waiting for my answer.

Okay, this isn't fair, I think. Jacob asks us all "why?" a hundred times a day and we all pick and choose when we should actually strive to give him a truly serious answer. I mean how can you really explain why the moon is round or the sun is hot or why grass sometimes feels scratchy and sometimes soft or why he can't grab the wooden chicken Nana keeps in the kitchen?

"Because..." I start looking for a way to explain.

Dad interrupts me. "If we teach him how to treat and respect toy guns, he'll know how to treat and respect a real gun," Dad says. "Look at him."

Jacob has lost interest in the conversation and his sandwich. He is now sitting back in his booster seat, swinging his legs, looking down the "barrel" of both hands as he holds them together in the shape of a gun and "shoots" at random objects around the kitchen. There's that whooshing sound again.

"Jake, we don't shoot guns at the table," Dad says again with a sterner voice. Jacob drops his hands willingly enough, says "Scuze me" and waits expectantly. We gladly excuse him from the table and he happily climbs down from his seat and runs off to play.

"See," Dad smiles. "Now he knows not to shoot guns at the table!" Dad gets up and pats my back as he walks by and heads for the garage.

Mother and I clear the table. "What do you think about all this?" I ask her.

"Well," she says, "you girls had toy guns when you were little. For a while, your guns were your favorite toys, along with your horses and your cowboy boots of course! And when you were older your Dad taught you how to shoot. And now you know. And you still seem to have a healthy respect for guns. " She starts laughing. "At least I don't see you waving any around as you shoot up the kitchen!"

Maybe they're right. Bottom line, I do not want Jacob brandishing weapons. So it makes sense I should teach him not to do so, not just forbid him from doing so. It doesn't quite make sense that the best way to teach him not to shoot guns is to give him a gun to play with as a toy, but he is making his own with or without my consent. Maybe I should go with the flow here and see what happens.

I join Jacob and Dad in the garage. Jacob is following Dad around pittering. Dad moves something here or there for some absent-minded reason and Jacob moves something else there and here for no other reason than because he just saw Dad do something similar. Wow. This role modeling is a powerful thing. A powerful, scary thing. Something one really doesn't want to mess up. Mom and Dad are both powerful role models for Jacob, but Dad has something Mother and I don't–a male perspective.

I remember after Jacob first learned to sit up, Dad would prop him up on his chair in the crook of his arm and rock back and forth singing, "Good ol' boys, that's all we are!" Before long, Jacob would be "singing" with him. "La, la, la, la, la..." Unknown gibberish voiced in the same pitch and cadence as Dad's song.

When Jacob was one year old, he would stand at the back storm door while Mother and I watched him watch Dad in the garage. He would bang on the door with his car-of-the-moment and say, "Da? Da-a-a!" More often than not, Dad would stick his head in the door, ask if Jacob could come out and play and let him join him in the garage for a while. Mother and I were never really sure what they did out there. Apparently they've been moving stuff around.

Jacob and I moved out of Mom and Dad's house when Jacob was about 18 months old. It was a rough transition. We have adjusted to living independently, but "Nana's house" is still Jacob's favorite place to be. And I am comfortable there as well. I trust my parents' parenting. It surprises me how many times I'm just really not sure what to do. And this gun thing is one topic about which I am grateful for some reinforcement.

I take a deep breath as if I'm about to step off the high dive. "Okay," I say, "he can have toy guns. But I need you to teach him how to use them and respect them. I need your help with this."

"Okay," Dad says, "you've got a deal." He gives me a wink.

New rules. Jacob can have toy guns at Nana and Hank's house

only. He is not allowed to bring them home or to play guns at our house or at friends' houses. He learns that guns are to be revered. He learns to not point them at people, to put them away, and to not shoot inside, much less at the dinner table.

Over the next few years, I watch Jacob and Dad's "gun play" mature and develop. When he is 5, they start making slingshots with forked branches and rubber bands—searching the woods for the perfect sling-shot stick becomes a favorite outing. And then, when Jacob is 7, a beloved BB gun appears. Jacob learns to load it, hold it, shoot it. They target shoot in the back yard together and off in the woods. And they traipse home happy, dirty and hungry, towing frogs and rocks and other found treasures–the modern version of the male hunt. I am always glad to see our "troops" come home. And I am glad they have each other and this time together in these woods.

JAN
May 2001

I work in the study for a couple hours and cry. I feel angry that Hank didn't clear out all these files. Then I remember he only had three weeks from the time he was diagnosed until we headed to Florida for treatment. During those three weeks, he spent many hours at this desk, but I don't think he was clearing out; I think he was trying to put things in order.

I remember him sitting in the front yard, short of breath, putting black rubber edging around the flowerbeds. I now understand he was facing his own mortality, realizing he might not survive the surgery, realizing he might never return to this house. When he did return, months later, he didn't have the energy or time to clear things out–he was just holding on.

And that's what I'm really mad about–I don't want him dead. I don't want to have to go through all the things in his study. I don't want to caulk the tub or sell the house or buy another one or move. I'm sad and tired and my shoulders hurt.

I see the female doctor at the clinic and tell her all the symptoms I have been having. "It sounds like you are suffering from a lack of estrogen," she says.

"Well, put me back on it!" I say without hesitating. She smiles and gently suggests we try some other things instead. I really like her.

I come in late and turn on the air conditioner. I am burning up with one hot flash after another. I am grateful the house has central air. I check the answering machine and my realtor's voice tells me she has scheduled an open house for Sunday. Maybe we will get a lot of look-ers. I grab my Jesus fan and start fanning.

The "For Sale" and "Open House" signs go up in the front yard. Jacob comes to help me get the yard and house ready for Sunday's open house. I remember how I grieved and cried when we put the Ohio house on the market when we were moving to Michigan. I loved that house and that neighborhood. I did not want to move. But we did and then three years later we moved here and this house in the woods became our favorite home. If this house sells, I have to believe I'll love another house and be happy again.

The realtor said a lot of people came through the open house and several seemed interested. Either way, I am enjoying a rare feeling of peace. I trust if I am to move, the house will sell and if I'm not to move, it won't. In the meantime, I will live in the moment. I will enjoy the familiarity, the screened porch, the woods, all the things Hank planted and the 20 years of memories that cradle me here. I feel the sudden need to get all my photographs in one place. Right now they are all over the house. I will get a trunk and tuck them all away in a safe place that I can take with me wherever I may go.

HANK

*(an original writing shared
with family years before his death)*

Love is an emotion directed toward an individual based on a deep rooted commitment or attachment.

Liking someone is a reaction to behavior based on one's past values and ideas of acceptable behavior.

It is therefore possible, in fact very likely, to love someone yet not like (disapprove) of a particular behavior.

The key is that one's dislike is of behavior, not the individual.

Since behavior is controlled by the individual and can be changed, our opinions of people change as their behavior becomes more acceptable or unacceptable to us.

Our love, however, remains constant.

It is a choice we continue to make,

Not a feeling with a life of its own over which we have no control.

CAMMIE
Memory 1988

I am trying to decide what I'm going to wear to work. Not much of a fashion diva, I usually don't give this decision too much thought. Good grief, what difference does it make? One-and-a-half-year-old Jacob is alone in the other room getting cranky. If I take too long, he may start throwing cans again.

Jacob and I moved out of Mom and Dad's house several months ago and into a rented house in a nearby town where I am working. He was so angry at first, that when I'd bring him from the babysitter's to our new home at the end of the day, he would grab cans out of the kitchen cabinets and throw them at my shins while I was cooking dinner. Ouch! It didn't take too many bruises before I decided to put those cans in the upper cabinets! Things are better now, but I figure we're still on a slippery slope; I can hear him beginning to whine in the other room. Just grab something to wear already! I finally put on a favorite dress and head towards the door. Get Jacob. Get my purse. Get the diaper bag. I seem to have everything...why do I feel like I'm missing something?

Distracted, I drive to the babysitter's house and drop Jacob off then head to work. I drive the same route, park in the same place and walk up the same stairs. But today I pause at the top before I open the door. What is this, this sense of something? I open the door and my eyes immediately meet those of an unfamiliar man standing in my boss' office who just happens to look up at that very moment. I can see him through the same glass walls that allow my boss to supervise the work floor.

I am working at a publishing house as the editor of a women's monthly magazine. The company publishes 18 magazines and employs a team of creative staff, production staff, sales staff and other support people. And today we appear to have a guest. I feel my heart skip a beat and my breath catches. What is that about? Embarrassed, I avert my eyes and find my way to my desk.

Later that morning, my boss gives the stranger a tour of the place. They eventually make their way over to me. "Allison, this is James," my boss says. "He has been working in the magazine industry in New York City and is going to be joining us as Art Director." I smile and say hello and extend my hand. He's not particularly attractive or articulate, but my nervous system is too busy doing gymnastics to notice that he doesn't say or do anything extraordinarily brilliant. What in the hell is wrong with me? I am practically shaking all over for goodness' sake! And apparently he's going to be working here...as my Art Director. Great, that's just great.

"Nice to meet you," I say and take my hand back. "I'm on a deadline," I smile in polite explanation, turn my attention back to my computer and hope he goes away.

But this is far from over. Over the next few weeks, James and I dance around each other at meetings and photo shoots and light boards. I find him to be more than a little arrogant and describe him to Mom and Dad as "that asshole from New York City who thinks he knows everything." But perhaps I protest too much. There is something else; something I can't name or overlook.

I find out he's 15 years older than me, divorced and has two daughters, Roma and Amanda, ages 8 and 9, who live with their mother in a city a couple of hours away. He moved back to Indiana to be closer to his girls. (My heart opens with a rush of compassion and warmth.) I discover he has a much better sense of design than I do and start seeking his opinion about various layouts. (My creative spirit bursts with inspiration.) During a brainstorming session, he asks the editorial team: Who is ready to take a risk? My hand spontaneously rises before I realize it is the only one up. (My sense of adventure sounds a silent battle cry that rings much louder than my embarrassment.) We share lunch one day and then I invite him over one evening and then he spends Saturday with Jacob and me and the next Sunday I go to meet his girls.

Mother comes over to visit. Well, actually she comes over to see Jacob, but that's okay. I'm still glad she's here. We try to talk over the corn popper push toy Jacob is proudly running around the living room. It was a surprise gift from my sister; I have since come to understand the glint in her eye when she gave it to him. With him demanding attention like this, the conversation is full of interruptions. Even so, I hear the name James popping out of my mouth over and over. And though I still don't know what that shaky feeling is, I do know it's more than I can negotiate; my only hope is to succumb.

Intuitive as she is, Mother goes home and tells Daddy she thinks I'm about to get married. "To whom?" he asks, surprised.

"To James," she answers.

"Isn't that the asshole from New York City who thinks he knows everything?"

"That's the one," she says. She invites us over for dinner. This is James' first trip to my parent's house and the first time he's met my Dad.

"Daddy," I say, "This is James." They shake hands.

"Nice to meet you," Daddy says.

"And we're getting married," I add. "Next week."

Mother smiles knowingly; Daddy looks somewhat aghast and turns to James. "Then it's really nice to meet you," he says. "And it sounds like we need to talk. And from the way she's telling it," he nods my way, "we don't have much time."

Daddy pours himself a drink, whisks James out to the back porch and lets Jacob scoot outside with them before he closes the sliding glass doors. Mother and I stay in the kitchen and finish preparing dinner.

"What do you think they're talking about out there?" I ask her, watching them through the glass.

"Oh, I don't know," she says. "Don't worry about them...talk to me. This all seems a little sudden. What's going on?"

"I know it's crazy," I say as I set the table. "I know I've only known him for six weeks. I can't really explain it. I just know we're supposed to be together."

"But why next week?" Mother asks as she puts the cornbread in the oven. "That certainly doesn't allow much planning time." She wipes her hands with a towel and runs water in the sink. "I mean, out-of-town family is probably going to want to come and certain arrangements need to be made...why do you need to get married next week?" She turns the water off and puts dishes in to soak.

I shrug. "I don't know," I say honestly. "There just doesn't seem to be any point in waiting." I start pouring water in the glasses. "I mean I planned a wedding with Henrie way in advance and look how that turned out. That was pretty much a disaster and all that planning proved to be a waste of time and money." I am looking out the window again. James and Daddy have moved off of the back porch and into the yard. They are both watching Jacob roll in the grass. James is looking a little pale.

"Maybe I should go out there," I think out loud.

"Just leave them alone for a while," she says. "We'll call them in when the cornbread's done." She takes the water pitcher out of my hand and sets it on the counter. Then she turns and pulls out a chair and pats the seat. "Now sit down and talk to me." She sits down in the chair next to mine. "This is a big decision," she points out. "Are you sure this is what you want?"

"Yes," I reassure her. "I can't explain it. It's like there's a magnet pulling me to him that I just can't resist." I recognize that worried look on her face. "Mother, you felt the same thing when you met Daddy," I remind her. "And you were only 16 when the two of you got married. You told everyone you were going to school, crossed the Mississippi state line, got married and didn't even tell anyone for three months! I'm a grown woman and I'm telling you ahead of time–only a week ahead, but at least I'm telling you!"

"Yes," she says, nodding her head. "You're right, you're a grown woman. With a little boy," she reminds me. "Have you thought about Jacob?"

Have I thought about Jacob? How can I not think about Jacob? Practically everything I do involves a thought about Jacob. Should I buy orange juice or apple juice? What should we do over the weekend? Should I stay up another hour reading or should I just go to bed so I'll be able to get up with Jacob in the morning? Should I watch this show on TV or that show or should I just turn it off? Should I take work home with me tonight or leave it for tomorrow so I can spend time with Jacob when I get home? Of course I've thought about Jacob!

The timer goes off letting us know the cornbread's done. Mother grabs the hot pad and moves for the oven door. She opens it up and the heat blasts her in the face. I catch her eye as she turns her head towards me, away from the onslaught. Time for closing arguments.

"Mom, I want Jacob to have a father in the house and I want a family. And I want to share that family with James. I don't need to wait for months to be sure and we don't want a big ceremony; we just want to start our lives together. Seems like we may as well start next week."

She reaches in and grabs the cornbread and sets it on the ready trivet. "Okay then," she says. "Go call the men. It's time to eat."

On the way home, I ask James what he and Daddy talked about while they were outside.

"Dad stuff Allison," he says dismissively. "He's just being your dad."

"But what did he say?" I persist.

"Basically, he told me he didn't have time to get to know me so he was going to cut through the bullshit and get to the point. He said if I ever hurt you or Jacob in any way that he would cloud up and rain all over me."

I turn around and look at Jacob who is asleep in his car seat. Good for Daddy, I think. I'm glad he's just being my dad.

At first we talk about having the wedding at Mom and Dad's house. Seems like as good a plan as any. But after a few days of them cleaning and prepping, I can think of several reasons why maybe that's not a great idea. So we decide to have it at the rental house where I am living. It has a huge yard and can hold a ton of people and chairs. When mother asks me what I plan to do about food, I spontaneously decide to make it a potluck event.

"You can't have a potluck wedding!" Mother says.

"Why not?" I ask. "People take potluck to summer picnics, why not a spring wedding? Instead of bringing a gift, they can bring food. And they can even take their dish back home with them!"

I can tell she's somewhat appalled, but I just really don't understand all the pomp and circumstance. I buy a dress and a crown of flowers for my hair. I get Jacob a miniature suit and some adorable saddle oxford shoes. I ask my sister to stand up with me and James asks his brother. Roma and Amanda join us and we have a full wedding party. Mom and Dad "give" us one of their early sets of wedding bands (they've replaced their wedding rings several times since their original dime store rings) on the condition that we have to give them back if our marriage dissolves. We get a minister and set out chairs. Friends gather. Daddy walks me down the sidewalk. James and I exchange vows on our wraparound porch and we all share food together. The party continues until late into the night. I go to bed blissfully happy and more than a little drunk.

The next morning I wake up with a hangover and am startled to find a man in my bed. But the surprises don't stop there. I walk out of my bedroom and am momentarily stunned to find two pre-teen girls on my couch and my house completely trashed. Always one to wake up a little slow, I look around trying to get oriented. What exactly happened here? Jacob is crying so I go get him out of bed, then stumble through the carnage into the kitchen looking for some painkiller to soothe my throbbing head so maybe I can think straight. Just in the nick of time too. Jacob is off and running with that stupid corn popper push toy. Oh, please, please, please stop making all that racket! By now James and the girls are awake–no one could sleep through all that noise–and all of us seem a little unsure about what to do next. All of us except Jacob...he is happily running that corn popper in circles around our confusion.

James' and Jacob's power struggle starts with that first corn popper run, but our transition as a family certainly lasts longer than those first awkward moments. James will tell Jacob to quit doing something and Jacob will completely ignore him. So James will put him in the corner and Jacob will raise his fist, shake it at him and scream, "No!" Brother. When Mom and Dad come to visit, Jacob runs down the sidewalk, climbs into their car and sits in the car seat, waiting patiently for them to take him to their house, regardless of whether they've planned on taking him with them or not. I keep a watchful eye on my son and a wary eye on my dad in case he decides to shape-shift into a cloud and start raining on this bizarre parody that has become my life.

The girls visit every other weekend. Eventually we move into a different house where they have their own room and no longer have to sleep on the couch. But this gesture only goes so far in bonding our relationship. At the end of the day, I am 25 years old and completely ill equipped to parent pre-teen girls. They already have two parents anyway, I remind myself. Maybe I shouldn't even try to be their parent...maybe there's a more appropriate role I can play. But I have no idea what that might be. And most of my fumbled attempts turn into screaming matches that reduce me to the status of their peer and leaves James shaking his head in bewilderment.

This trend continues for a few years until one summer when I strike a deal with Roma who I am convinced keeps her nose in a book so she has a handy excuse to ignore me. I decide to meet her where she's at. I suggest we pick a book for each other to read, then discuss it when we're done. I must have piqued her curiosity because she cautiously agrees. I pick *Clan of the Cave Bear* by Jean Auell for her first read. Once she gets started, she's hooked. She eventually reads her way through the entire Earth's Children's series giving us about 3,000 pages of historical fiction to discuss and building a foundation for a relationship that eventually ventures beyond reading material. And amazingly enough, once Amanda sees Roma give me the benefit of the doubt, she readily follows suit. Thank goodness.

But even in the midst of all this chaos, I am happy. We are happy. Daddy loans us money to buy computers and I start working for the publishing company out of my house as a contractor. I quit sending Jacob to the babysitter and happily learn how to work and be a stay-at-home mom. A few years later we move to Fort Wayne and buy a rambling, run-down pink Victorian house with a porch swing, a turret and a deck on the second floor. We designate an office area and launch our own design business. Money is tight, but life is good. It may take a little longer than it takes to cook a pan of cornbread to figure it all out, but I am comforted and encouraged by the promise of a bright future full of possibilities. I am living in love.

JAN
May 2001

When I began considering this move, I was controlled by fear. I was afraid of letting go and I was afraid of moving on. I was so afraid of losing this peaceful haven, I was not able to focus on what I may gain if I move. I will have less house to clean, no stairs, a newer home with less maintenance. I make a choice to put my thoughts in order and to focus on the positive. I make a choice to listen to my heart. I will not move to a place that is not right for me. I need trees and shade and nature. If I move, I will find a place where I can live surrounded by trees.

I feel more strongly that I want to build on a wooded lot in the subdivision in town. I feel at home every time I drive by. I begin visualizing myself living there. I talk to the financial advisor with whom Hank worked. I meet with the builder. I give him a check for earnest money. If my house sells, I will get an apartment and store my furniture while I build a new house. I am really ready for my house to sell. They are showing it a lot. I feel uneasy, as if I am slipping on ice, as if I have no traction, as if I can't quite get a grip. I have never liked the state of limbo, but I think I'm handling it pretty well. I am perched on the edge of a high cliff, ready to soar. I could fall, but I don't think I will. I think I'll fly! How far I have come.

Hank was always so supportive and encouraging and tolerant of me. He never yelled at me when I did stupid things. He didn't yell at me the day I called him out of a meeting at work to tell him the car had been stolen out of the parking lot at the mall.

"I have walked up and down aisle after aisle in the parking lot in the pouring rain!" I cried into the phone. "And the car isn't here. Somebody must have stolen it!"

He came and picked me up. "Are you okay?" he asked me as I get into the car, soaking wet.

"I'm so sorry!" I wailed.

"Well, don't be," he said. "I never liked that car anyway! I'm glad it's been stolen. All the way over I've been thinking about what kind of car we should buy to replace it. What do you think?" he asked excitedly as he drove around the parking lot. "What entrance did you come in anyway?" He headed in the direction I was pointing. I guided him down the lane where I had parked and we suddenly drove by our car.

"They brought it back!" I said in surprise.

"Hell yes they brought it back," he grumbled. "They didn't like it either!"

It appeared the car had not been stolen after all. Unaccustomed to navigating around large shopping malls, I had entered through one door and exited through another and that put me in a different parking lot. But Hank didn't criticize me for such a foolish mistake; he just laughed and said he had a story to tell for years.

Hank died 18 months ago today. During this time I have been disoriented, unable to get my bearings, not sure if I am coming or going. Oh, the places this journey of grief has taken me! At times, it has almost felt as if my very life essence has been stolen. I have traveled in valleys so low, through tunnels so dark I couldn't see my next step. I have inched my way up mountains high and slippery, knowing with each fear-gripping step that if I lost my footing I would fall so far and so deep I may never be found. I have leaned against friends and family who sturdily provided brief periods of respite.

I have reflected on my life with Hank and relived joyous moments as well as our heart-wrenching last days. I have accepted that such love and companionship may be forever gone and have hoped for the chance to experience that kind of love yet again. I have embraced love and pain and loss. I have dug through, thrown out, hung on, clung to and let go. I have clenched and released and opened. I have traveled unmarked territory, danced new steps alone and have finally learned to float.

This journey has shaken the roots of who I am and what I believe. My identity was so intertwined with Hank's, I was more of a "we" than a "me." I have gotten to know myself well–I have become my own traveling companion.

June 2001

Daddy calls crying. His friend Gwen died today. The funeral is hard on both of us. Afterwards, we go out to eat and he asks, "What do you think your mother is doing?"

"I think she's waiting for you Daddy. I think she's been waiting a long time."

He nods his head yes. "Hon, I'm not a bit afraid to die," he says quietly. "In fact, I'm ready."

"I know, but I'll miss you when you leave," I answer. Quiet tears run down my face. I know my days on earth with my daddy are few. This is so hard. I'm tired of people dying. I'm tired of being lonely. But I am so grateful for the chance to talk with him about real feelings.

He tells me how much he misses Mother and his home in Kentucky. It was really brave of him to move up here to an assisted living home near us. I hate to see him have to go through much more. I wish he could just go to sleep and not wake up. We talk about Hank and Mother. We talk about how his spirit body won't need a walker. Every time I see Daddy he is thinner. He walks slower and slower. Little by little he is disappearing.

I remember years ago when Daddy still lived in Kentucky and had an appointment in Nashville, Tennessee for heart by-pass surgery. We drove down and spent a couple of days with him before taking him to Nashville. He was so weak and frail. Hank and I stepped out onto the porch one evening and he cried. He said he didn't think Daddy would make it through the surgery and he wasn't ready to let him go. When mother died, we drove 12 hours to get to them. Soon after our arrival, Hank called his mother to tell her, but was crying so hard he couldn't talk. Hank would be sad now if he saw Daddy like this.

I invite Carl and his wife Shirley to go with me to take Daddy out to dinner. Daddy really likes Carl. Carl prays with him and they talk about spiritual things. Daddy rarely ever gets to visit with a man. We pull up and Daddy is on the porch. "Hey Daddy, how are you?" I ask. He looks tired. "I'm worn out from trying to get my funeral clothes together," he says. "Will you go in and hang them up for me?" Shirley and I go to his room. It takes just a few minutes to hang his clothes.

Since Gwen died, Daddy mainly talks about his funeral. He says he is weary; I think his spirit is broken. He seems to be living more on the other side than here on earth. The nurse tells me he has been falling backwards a lot. She says they have not seen anyone else do that. They encourage him to drink more water, go to physical therapy and eat a banana every day. He complains the nurses are on him about not eating and losing weight. I tell him if he is wanting to die, that's one way to do it, but if he wants to live he needs to eat. He orders a chili dog and milk shake and eats every bite.

July 2001

I'm having an off day. I feel so lonely. I am 60 years old. What does life hold for me? I wish I had a date tonight. Hank and I had "date" nights often. I miss that so much. Sometimes, while enjoying an evening at home, Hank would put on music and ask me to dance. One night, when Cammie was in college, she went out for the evening and came home much earlier than expected. She caught us dancing in the family room, scantily clad with lights out and candles burning. She came in the door and said, "What's going on? Oh….never mind. I'm going upstairs to bed. Good night!" The longer we were married, the more we seemed to love and enjoy each other.

I sit on the screened porch and drink in the hushed woods, the distant noise of mowers and airplanes, the humming of birds at the feeder, the chattering of squirrels. I sit here and remember all the love this house has held. I remember visiting children and grandchildren and welcoming Cammie and baby Jacob with his black stand-up hair to come live with us—I can still hear him as a toddler pounding on the back door, watching Hank in the garage and yelling, "Daaa!"

I remember dinner parties with dear friends, making love, cooking meals, watching movies, listening to music, slow dances... I remember feeling special to another human being and feeling loved and accepted. I can still see Hank in the yard weeding or sitting on this porch working crossword puzzles. And I remember the living room turned into a chamber of death: the tears, the grief, the fear, the lonely hours. And now, there are new beginnings.

All these things this house has known. I wonder what my future holds. Will this house sell? Will I make another home? Will I move into a blank slate that holds no memories of us or him? Or will I remain here and somehow manage to blend what was and what is into what will be? All I know is that I know nothing. Nothing is certain. This much-loved porch now sits on shifting sand that moves with an unknown tide. I cry for what I've lost and for what might be—for a new life full of new memories.

CAMMIE
Dream Summer 2001

I am walking down the street in a hurry. I am having problems finding my way. I am confused, disoriented, distressed. Am I in Chicago? Fort Wayne? Hong Kong? I hear a loud, male voice directing me. I am trying to locate it, but it has no source. It is everywhere and nowhere—it is disembodied. But it is giving me directions, telling me where to go, so I listen and take heed. Turn here, turn there. The voice leads me to a subway portal. I go down the stairs and am standing at a turnstile, hesitant to enter, not wanting to commit. "Take the subway!" The voice booms. So I do. I get on the subway train and take a seat.

I am the only one on the train. The world outside the window races by in a blur. Sometimes the train is below ground and I see only darkness. Sometimes the train is above ground and I see a whirlwind of color and shapes, but I can't make sense of any of the images. I am blindly traveling through as if I am being carried in a womb. Inside the subway car, the temperature is controlled; the seats are comfortable. I nap, I eat, I read. I am grateful for the opportunity to be still and rest. When I finally get bored, the train stops. I am as hesitant to get off as I was to get on. Where am I? I stand at the open door, unsure. "Get off the train!" The voice booms. So I do.

I take the stairs to the street and emerge at a familiar intersection in Fort Wayne. I look up into a blue sky as a bright sun warms my skin. A soft breeze carries the song of birds and the lively banter of people. A man sitting across the street smiles and beckons me over. As I get closer, I see it is Daddy. I run up and hug him. "What are you doing here?" I ask. "I am so happy to see you!"

He pats me on the back. "I just want you to know how proud of you I am," he says. "You're doing a good job." There's that voice. It was his voice directing me!

I burst into tears. "I'm tired all the time," I say.

"I know," he nods.

"And I'm afraid. Half the time I have no idea what to do."

He nods again and gets up as if to leave.

That's it? That's all he has to say? The man has traveled beyond and back and all he offers is a nod?

He starts to walk away, then turns. "You don't have to always know up here." He taps his head. "Just pick a direction, then go along and enjoy the ride." He turns away and disappears.

JAN
August 2001

I have lost all interest in this house. When Hank was alive and I was living my other life, I enjoyed decorating and making the house homey and pretty. Now it's just a bunch of clutter that has to be dusted. All the collections that used to mean so much to me, I wish I could pack them all away. I need to simplify.

I remember how I needed to wear Hank's things after he died. I wore the gold necklace he gave me, his rings, his watch and some of his clothes. I wouldn't wash his pillowcase because it still held his scent. Now I only wear my diamond on my right hand. I have put most of his pictures away. I can go up to his study and pay bills at his desk without crying.

I'm at such a strange crossroads. I'm sure I will walk through this passage as I have others. I'm probably depressed about the house not selling and dread another autumn with so many leaves to rake. If it weren't for Daddy and Cammie and the kids, I might move back home to Mayfield, Kentucky.

The nurse calls and says Daddy has lost 18 pounds in the past six months and he was already too thin. She says they have noticed a big change in him since Gwen died. I told her he wants to die, that his funeral is now our main topic of conversation.

I receive an offer on the house. I have four days to respond. It's not what I wanted, but I talk to my financial advisor and decide to accept the offer. The buyers want me out by September 25. That feels manageable to me. I'll have plenty of time to pack. I talk to the builder and he should be able to start my new house in the fall and have me in it by April. I go sign papers and it's a done deal–the house is sold. I feel at peace and am happy.

I reserve a moving date with the movers. Carl brings me boxes. Don comes over for coffee. He is proud of me for taking control of my life. Diane talks to friends who have a garage apartment they will let me rent for six to seven months. Daddy sells his car.

It is a terribly hot day. I pack awhile and rest awhile. I try to clear a path in the living room and organize all the boxes. Salvation Army comes and takes away a lot of things. I lay out piles for the girls. I don't have time to think or reflect—I'm working too hard physically. My hip and back are beginning to hurt from all the bending and lifting. I'm so thankful I've been able to do all this packing without burdening my kids. Cammie and the kids have helped some, but mainly I'm doing it and it feels good.

The realtor calls and the buyers have decided they want me out by September 5. That moves things up by about three weeks. I will have to work much harder and longer each day to meet that deadline. I can move into the apartment earlier than planned, but won't have phone service for two weeks.

Carl offers to help me empty the storage area over the garage. It is awfully hot, but we get it done. Now I have to go through all those boxes and decide what to keep and what to get rid of. I clean up and go to the closing on the house. I put Hank's framed picture on the desk by me as I sign the papers. We bought this house years ago with much joy and anticipation. We had each other. I'm now leaving it behind and moving on. I hope he is proud of me.

I come in hot and rest for a while. The nurse calls to tell me Daddy had to go to the hospital by ambulance. I hurry to the closing on the lot and then go to the hospital. I am in the emergency room with him until he is finally admitted at 1 a.m. The tests show a bowel obstruction. Early the next morning Diane and I go to the hospital and get there just as they are taking him to surgery to repair a hernia in the groin. Cammie and the kids and Carl and Shirley and John and Diane all wait with me. We are amazed he makes it through the surgery okay. For the next several days, I pack in the mornings and evenings and visit him in the afternoons. I am definitely stressed.

I think about other times when life felt overwhelming and solutions were not apparent. I remember the winter Babs was a year old. Hank went out to warm up the car and came in cold and shivering.

"Bad news Jan," he said. "The heater in the car isn't working."

"Oh no!" I cry. "What are we going to do?"

"What can we do?" he says. "We don't have the money to get it fixed. I guess we'll just have to bundle up. Make sure you put Babs in extra clothes and wrap her up in blankets!" We spent that entire winter driving around without a car heater. By the next fall, we had saved a little extra money and decided to get it fixed. When Hank took the car in, we found out all it needed was a 25-cent fuse! We laughed about that cold winter and that "expensive" car repair for years.

I don't want to lose perspective in the midst of this sea of change. Just because things might feel insurmountable, doesn't mean they are. Sometimes it's just about putting one foot in front of the other; sometimes the solution is as simple as a 25-cent fuse.

CAMMIE
August 2001

I rush into the car rental place, bringing the hot air with me into the air-conditioned room. "I need to keep my rental car for another week," I explain to the man behind the counter.

"Ah, Allison," the man says walking towards the customer service desk. I'm a little startled. I didn't realize that Gary (the tag on his shirt says his name is Gary) knew my name. Of course, I was in several times the previous week. My old beat up Subaru is on its last legs and is in the shop. I am finishing the last few weeks of my summer fieldwork assignment in Chicago and am desperate for transportation. I came in the first time last week asking for a good rate on a rental car for a few days. My budget doesn't allow much room for the unexpected and it certainly doesn't allow for extensive rentals of expensive cars. I came in needing a cheap car for a few days. Simple enough.

But then the mechanics working on my Subaru reported they were having problems and it was going to take more time and cost more money...so I went back to the rental car place a second time to see if I could keep the car longer. And to negotiate the cost below their normal rate, somehow trying to make it fit within my precariously unbalanced budget. Now the mechanics are saying my Subaru still isn't done and probably won't be done until next week. So I'm back again. Good grief. Gary doesn't seem particularly happy to see me.

"I need to keep my rental car for another week," I say again. "But I don't need it the whole week. How about I keep it on your lot and only actually rent it from midnight Monday to midnight Tuesday and from midnight Wednesday to midnight Thursday?"

I figure that way I can get to Chicago on Tuesday and Thursday as needed without having to pay for a full week's rental. I have no idea who is going to give me a ride to and from the rental car place at midnight or how I'll get around the rest of the week, but I have learned to only focus on one thing at a time. Planning and prevention appear to be luxuries I can no longer afford; the demands for my time, attention and money keep hitting me faster than my limited resources can keep up. The best I can do is triage and try to tend to whatever problem is screaming the loudest at any given moment.

"If you still need the car, why don't you just keep it for the week?" Gary sounds slightly annoyed. I probably would be too if I saw myself from a well-planned, well-ordered perspective based in a world of plenty.

"Because I can't afford a whole week's rental," I say bluntly. I am way beyond shame.

Gary holds my gaze for a moment as if considering. "Your car is in the shop, right?" I nod yes.

"Didn't they tell you it was going to be ready last week?" he asks.

I nod again. "Yes, but I guess they're having some problems with it."

"What kind of problems?" he asks.

Good grief. I don't know. Problem problems. The kinds of problems mechanics have when they work on cars. How am I supposed to know?

"I'm not sure," I say, shrugging my shoulders. Gary is still looking at me.

"Maybe you should have your husband call and talk to them about your car," he suggests. Great idea Gary, but that leads us to yet another problem.

"I don't have a husband," I say flatly.

"Well, then your boyfriend," he says, shaking his head and gesturing, obviously annoyed by details that are beside the point. Clearly, his point is I should ask whatever man is in my life to talk to the mechanic.

"Look," I say, suddenly embarrassed. "There is no one to make that call. I mean, there was someone..." Why am I embarrassed? Why do I feel the need to explain? "I was married. But then we separated and then we divorced. And then he died. Suddenly and unexpectedly..." I start crying. "He died last Christmas Eve!" Now I'm wailing. "I still can't believe he died on Christmas Eve!" And now Gary seems embarrassed too. Poor Gary.

"Well, maybe your Dad could call and talk to the mechanic," he says quietly. He no longer sounds annoyed; his tone is beginning to twinge with compassion.

Oh boy, here we go, I can feel it coming... is he ever going to be sorry he said that! I involuntarily rest my elbows on the counter and hold my head in my hands while great sobs wrack through my whole body.

"Daddy's dead too!" I cry. "He died the year before! They're both dead and I'm trying to finish graduate school in Chicago while I live and work and raise kids here in Fort Wayne!" I'm beyond embarrassed. I'm pathetic.

Gary must be afraid to say anything else because he waits in silence until I regain some composure. He hands me the tissue box from his desk and asks quietly, "Allison, where is your car and what kind of car is it?"

I tell him and he looks up the number in the phone book. He dials the shop and says, "This is Mr. Ballard calling about the Subaru that my wife brought in last week. I've been on a business trip and just got home and discovered the car is still not ready for pick up. I had understood it was supposed to have been ready last week. I'm not happy to find that she's still driving a rental car. I need an update on the Subaru's status and need to know when it's going to be finished."

Go Gary! The conversation goes back and forth on the phone. Mechanical banter appears to be a language my new husband speaks. "Okay," I hear him say. "So she should be able to pick it up this afternoon? Great! And if you have any problems, could you please call me at this number? Thank you. Goodbye."

Gary gets off the phone and hands me his business card. "Allison, if your car isn't ready for you this afternoon, give me a call," he says.

He comes around the counter and pats me on the back. "It's okay," he says reassuringly. "Everything is going to be okay."

I resist the impulse to bury my head in his chest. Instead, I mumble thank you and walk back out into the sweltering heat.

JAN
September 2001

I work hard over the weekend. I give away the family room furniture. Hank's chair is now gone. I feel like I'm losing more of him with this move. I work in the back yard gathering up bird feeders, statues etc. That's where I see and feel Hank the most. Even good things can hurt. Surgery hurts, but it also heals.

It is moving day. Four nice, hardworking men come at 8 a.m and leave at 1 p.m. to take things to storage. Diane helps me vacuum after they leave, then goes to the apartment with me to put shelf paper down. I work in the apartment for several hours, then get my shower and just sit. It feels good to just sit for awhile.

Sitting in front of the fan in my new apartment I realize I am beginning a new chapter, flying solo. This is the first place I have lived in 44 years that Hank has not shared with me. There is no memory of him here, nor will there be in the new house. I remind myself that a clenched fist cannot grab hold of new wonderful things. If I'm tightly holding on to the past, I can't grab the future. I have to let go of my old life to embrace my new life. I feel at peace here. The bed seems a little strange at first, but I will adapt. I hope to settle into my new house and live many happy, healthy years. Maybe by my 61st birthday next week I'll be unpacked and settled.

I go to the house for the last time and leave the keys. I speak out loud. "Hank, this is my last time at this house. We are moving on!" I back out of the driveway without crying or looking back. I am not leaving his spirit here; I am taking it with me. I have packed it in my heart.

Hank died 22 months ago today. It seems like a lifetime ago. I feel so tired. Today feels like the first day in weeks that I can slow down and take it easy. This apartment has a metal roof and I love hearing the rain hit it. My phone service won't start for two weeks. Not having a phone seems so strange. In one way I feel cut off and isolated–but it's also kind of like being in a cocoon, sheltered from the world.

I go to a pay phone and call Daddy to remind him of an upcoming business appointment. He was confused and had the dates mixed up. I ask if he has all the papers together and he isn't sure so I tell him I will come early and help him. He is really slipping.

I work hard for a short time today, but don't push myself. I feel myself letting down from all the stress of the past few months. My adrenalin has been pumping for weeks and now I'm beginning to relax. I was lying in bed this morning thinking of all the places I've called home since April 1998 when Hank first got sick. We turned motel rooms and hospital rooms and the little Florida apartment into a home. "Home is where the heart is" and my heart was where Hank was. When I look back on the last three years, I am stunned by all the adaptations we made. The human spirit is amazing.

Life is an adventure! It's like reading a good book–you never know what the next page will reveal and sometimes, after you've read the last page, you are disappointed that it is over because you enjoyed the experience of reading it so much. I am here alone in this new home, looking forward to the next page.

It is September 11, 2001, an awful day in the history of our country. Hi-jacked planes hit the World Trade Center towers and the Pentagon. Another one crashes in a field in Pennsylvania. I pick Daddy up and we take care of our business appointment. Everywhere I go, people are talking about the disaster. I come in with a headache.

September 12 is my birthday; I turn 61 and watch TV all day, catching news about the terrorist attacks. It breaks my heart to think about all the grief all these families will go through. The news tells me that the destroyed buildings in New York City had asbestos in them. I watch the people on TV breathe in all that dust. I wonder how many cases of mesothelioma will result.

The air feels like fall and reminds me of Hank's struggle to live. The news shows a picture of a young man on one of the planes who called his wife with his last words, "I love you." Those were Hank's last words to me. What would mine be and who would I call? At WalMart, a manager calls on the intercom for a moment of respectful silence for the victims and their families. There is not a sound in the whole store. It is eerie. I stand in an aisle alone and sob.

And still, life goes on. The world is chaos, Hank is dead, I am alone and there is nothing I can do about any of it. I cook my first meal here in my small, cozy apartment. I feel strangely safe and strangely happy! I'm going to enjoy my time living in this little apartment that is easy to keep clean and straight. I have a good book to read and a new piece of cross-stitch to work on. Tomorrow, I will go to the laundromat for the first time in many years.

October 2001

I drive to Lexington, Kentucky then on to Mayfield. I spend time with cousins and friends and a long time at Hank's grave. I go home and meet the builder at the lot. He shows me where the rooms will be and which trees will have to be cut. They will break ground soon. I have drawn the house and my furniture to scale on graph paper and am playing around with the furniture arrangement. I feel like a little girl playing with a new doll house!

It is cold, windy and rainy. I stay in and do needlework and read. It feels good to be able to relax. This apartment has a day bed and a sofa bed in the living room so the kids have a place to sleep when they come spend the night. I love having a bed in the living room. It feels good not to have a big two-story house to take care of. I love spending my days in this little apartment. I like this time in my life. I am my own good company. I entertain myself well. I know who I am. I know where I have been and trust where I am going.

I drive by the lot and take pictures. They have cut some trees and are digging. They are laying the foundation. I meet some of my new neighbors. I feel so blessed to have my health and enough money to live comfortably and to build a small home in a beautiful setting. I am so grateful to have a loving family, inner peace and strong spiritual faith. I am grateful for beautiful memories of a wonderful marriage and to have come this far in my grief journey.

CAMMIE

Memories 1990-1991

I move my big belly slowly through the house, glancing out the window at the swirling snow. There is a blizzard blowing and I am on a deadline. I am 6 months pregnant and am preparing to put my baby belly and 4-year-old Jacob in the car and drive all three of us through this storm to deliver some work that must be handed off by tomorrow morning. I am afraid. And angry. Where is James? Why must I do this by myself? Why must I take Jacob with me? If James was here, I could leave Jacob with him and then at least I would have one child safe.... better yet, if James was here he could go out in this storm and I could stay home safe and sound with Jacob and baby.

I waddle through our large Victorian gathering blankets and work files and some toys to entertain Jacob. "Where is he?" I rant, slamming the closet door behind me. "How can anyone be expected to drive safely in this weather?" I rave, stuffing things into a tote bag. Jacob is following me through every room, down the hall, around each corner. In my maddened haste, I cut the corner short and bang my distended belly on the door frame. "I tell you one thing," I bluster, "if I arrive home safely, I may not drive the rest of the winter! He may just have to chauffeur me around!"

I continue ranting and raving, venting my anger and fear until Jacob suddenly yells, "Stop!" His voice is not anxious or plaintive; it is commanding and clear.

I turn and look. My son stands before me, a juxtaposition of tender innocence and seasoned wisdom. He looks at me dead on with an intensity I do not recognize. His spine stands tall on short legs. His "di," the cloth diaper he carries with him everywhere, hangs from his clenched fist that is poised mid-air. His thumb is still sticking up from where he pulled it suddenly from its beloved place in his mouth. His hair sticks up as well, an untamed mohawk I can never comb down.

I stop as commanded, but the fight isn't out of me yet. "What?" I snap, annoyed.

"Don't you know I love you like the wind rushing over the water?" Buddha boy asks me, then pops his thumb back into his mouth and morphs back into being just a little boy.

Dumbfounded, I watch his jaw work as he sucks hard on his thumb through the suspended silence. His unspoken words ring clearly between us. "What is the matter with you? Why are you rampaging through the house like a madwoman? Don't you know how much I love you? What could possibly be wrong if we love each other this much?"

I melt onto the floor. "Come here," I say quietly and hold out my arms. He runs to me and I cradle him against my pregnant belly. We sit quietly, rocking together for a long time. I can hear the wind howling. He may have melted me with his innocent wisdom, but the blizzard is still swirling outside and I am still on a deadline.

I heave myself up off the floor and say with forced excitement, "We're going on an adventure! You, the baby and me!" We put on coats and boots and I carry him to the car.

The snow has long since melted by the time my water breaks several months later. It is a beautiful day in May. I have been planning a home birth for months and I am ready for this baby to be born! I call the midwife and my mother and James' mother and Roma and Amanda. And then I wait. Why isn't anything happening? A friend drives me to a nearby park and we walk. The flowers are beautiful and the sky is clear blue...it is indeed a beautiful day to have a baby–if I would just have a contraction already. My friend drives me back home and I wait some more.

It seems like I have been waiting forever to meet this baby girl who is about to come into our world. Before she was even a thought in my head, this powerful unnamed, unknown spirit rode on my left shoulder and whispered in my ear asking to be conceived.

After several weeks of trying to ignore it, I realized it wasn't going anywhere. "I think it's time we have a baby," I finally said to James and my shoulder grew quiet. About halfway through the pregnancy we decided to name her Allison Jade if she was a girl. A beautiful name I was excited to give her. As it ends up, she had other thoughts.

"India." I hear it as a whisper in my dream. I am alone in a white room with no walls and no corners. It isn't really a room at all–I am alone in a brilliantly white void. "India," says the whisper.

"What?" I look around, trying to catch the word or at least identify its source. "Who are you?"

"India," it says again, repeating itself over and over until it becomes many voices chanting. "India, India, India..." The voices grow louder and louder until they are booming, spinning me around. "India! India! India!" I wake up. I have never heard of India as a name, but there is no mistake.

"This baby is a girl," I announce to James, shaking him out of sleep. "And her name is India. I hope you like it."

Of course, we liked the name we had already picked out. So we settle for a compromise (the first of many!) with this strong little soul and decide to name her India Allison Jade Ballard-Bonfitto. It's not a name; it's a novel. She'll carry her entire life story on her driver's license. If she's ever born, that is.

Contractions finally start late afternoon. Another round of phone calls to family and then a light dinner and by early evening I realize I better get up the stairs while I still can or I might end up having this baby on the kitchen floor. I slowly get up into bed and the midwife comes. She checks me, checks the room, checks that we have everything on hand as we have been instructed.

"Everything looks good," she assures us. "Wake me up when you need me."

She promptly goes downstairs to "nap" on the couch, explaining she was up the previous night with an early morning birth. Hey, I need you right now! I think as the contractions start coming faster. I reach for something to hold onto and find James hand. I squeeze hard, look for a focal point and concentrate on my breathing.

If I was expected to birth this baby in silence they would have to kill me, because before too long I have had enough of breathing. Without any medication, it feels like I am being split apart–maybe this home birth wasn't such a good idea after all. I start "vocalizing" my way through each contraction and then I am flat out screaming.

"I am never doing this again!" becomes my mantra.

While resting in between, I ask about Jacob. Mother brings him into my room; he is wearing his batman pajamas, cape intact, di in hand, thumb in mouth.

"Don't be afraid," I tell my little superhero before I am swallowed by another wave of pain. Mother whisks him off to a nearby room where she rocks him in her lap. This is one moment I am grateful Jacob was born deaf in one ear...with his good ear pinned to Mother's chest, he is soothed by the resonance of her voice; his exposed deaf ear remains blissfully oblivious to the sounds of his sister coming into the world.

At 5:55 in the morning, India is born: healthy, beautiful and bald. A sleepy, curious Jacob crawls in bed beside me to get a good look. India is examined and weighed and put to my breast. I am exhausted and happy; my family is complete. (I really am never doing this again!)

India is asleep and I want to do the same–after I have a shower. The midwife and my mother change the bed while I go into the bathroom. Apparently, I fail to hear her instruction about avoiding hot water because one minute I am thinking how good the warm water feels and the next I am on the bathroom floor looking up at worried faces. It appears the hot water caused me to hemorrhage and I passed out in the shower; the sound of my fall brought everyone rushing in. A few drops of capsicum under my tongue stops the bleeding and fortunately I'm not injured in the fall so, except for giving everyone quite the scare, all is well. Until later that day.

After hours of activity, the house is finally quiet. Roma and Amanda and James' mother have all come and gone. Mother has taken Jacob home with her and James has finally left to go borrow a shovel and bury the placenta–a task unique to the home birth experience. India is asleep and I am enjoying my solitude until I start having labor pains. How can this be possible? I've never heard of a twin being born hours later....nonetheless, my body refuses reason and goes into a contraction. I crawl into the bathroom and lay down on the floor. A few minutes later I give birth to...something.... something dark brown and about the size of a small football...my newborn daughter's twin is a football? My mind races through the homebirth classes James and I had to take. Leaving the football where it lay, I hoist myself up off the floor and go call Mother.

"Mother, I think my uterus just fell out," I say calmly.

"What are you talking about?" she asks uncomprehendingly. "I thought it was hooked in there with something!"

I explain what happened. "I learned in birthing class that a possible complication to childbirth is a prolapsed uterus," I remember.

"I don't think that means your uterus can fall out!" she says.

"Well, mine has," I answer matter-of-factly. "I'm the exception."

"Surely not," she says. "Maybe you need to go to the hospital."

"There is no way I'm going to the hospital!" I say emphatically. "If I do, they're just going to want to put it back in. And I'm tired of things being pushed and pulled in and out of me. I don't need it anymore anyway. I'm just going to have James bury it in the back yard with the placenta."

"Oh, Cammie!" Mother cries. "I think you should at least call the midwife and talk to her and figure out what's going on. You have two kids to take care of now; you have to take care of yourself!"

"Okay," I sigh, burdened with the responsibilities of motherhood. Oh, for the days I could just throw my uterus away and no one would care! I call the midwife and describe my newborn football, aka uterus. She chuckles and gives it yet another name: a blood clot, more than likely resulting from my earlier hemorrhaging. Laughing, she assures me I do not have to go to the hospital and have it put back in. James buries it in the back yard, whatever it is. And the ferns grow splendidly thereafter.

As does the garden. During pregnancy, I was struck with a blight of domesticity and worked with friends to plant my first garden. Through the spring, my daily routine was to go out every evening after dinner and work in the garden while Jacob played outside. Then we would come in for bath and stories and bedtime.

Needless to say, the birth of India Jade has disrupted our routine; I haven't worked in the garden in awhile. But tonight is the night. I feel good; India is asleep and the garden certainly needs some attention. I collect my gloves, a gathering basket and some gardening tools. I carry India in her infant seat and put her on the back porch so I can hear her if she cries. Jacob runs off to play with friends. It feels good to dig in the dirt. It feels good to stretch and bend and gently work my sore, no-longer-pregnant body.

The sun goes down and dusk falls. I gather my tools and call Jacob. We go inside and I start his bath. Why does it feel like I am forgetting something? I make him a snack and he picks out a bedtime story. This nagging feeling hangs on like a baby nursing at my breast. Oh my goodness, the baby! I forgot the baby! I run out the back door with my heart pounding. There she is, asleep in her infant seat on the back porce, safe and sound and alone in the dark. I am so relieved I am crying. It's going to take some time to get used to this new addition to our family. But India Jade soon begins to leave her mark.

"How is little Jade?" my mother asks me on the phone.

"Oh, she's so sweet," I coo. "Every night I put her in her infant swing while I cook dinner and she does such sweet mudras with her hands. Her finger movements are so intricate and precise!" I brag, choosing not to mention that I can't get her to reach for a toy. Good thing her fine muscle development is so advanced because her large muscle development is as lacking as her hair.

"What are mudras?" my mother asks.

"They're symbolic hand gestures used in Indian dance," I explain. "Maybe she was an East Indian dancer in a past life. Or perhaps she was a monk which would explain her bald head. Either way, I guess she knew what she was doing when she named herself India."

"Hmmm..." my mother says. She still refuses to call her India. I think the name is a little too farfetched for her even though I point out the precedent she set by naming her three girls Babs, Lita and Cammie! (Good grief! Try explaining that!) It's not until a friend shows my mother a magazine article about the name India published in a Southern Living magazine that she finally gets on the bandwagon. Apparently, India is an old southern name; there's even a character in Gone With the Wind named India. (Who would have known?) Once this piece of trivia is learned, my mother brags to all her friends that she has a granddaughter named India!

Yes, India has certainly carved her way into our hearts and our lives. With blue eyes, light skin and blonde fuzz, she is as fair as Jacob is dark. My high contrast children are perfect complements of each other with easygoing natures, curious intellects and creative sparks that fill my life with one chaotic, joyful moment after another. Throw Roma and Amanda and our work-at-home business into the mix, and James and I have every reason to feel blessed.

Except that money is always tight and the house is falling apart around us and we disagree about almost everything. Except for all that, our life is perfect bliss.

HANK

(found in his desk after his death)

PRINCIPLES TO LIVE BY

1. Always strive to give more than you receive.
2. You cannot manage people; you can only lead.
3. No matter how important you believe you become, God is always bigger.
     Learn to love and trust God.
4. Always manage to save a little money.
5. Always think and act as if you had no money.
6. Always be true to yourself in everything you do.
7. Things that don't change stay the same.
8. Be conservative in your dress and your appearance.
9. Face all things with a positive attitude.
10. Have a plan for your life and work hard at that plan.
     Change as necessary.

JAN
November 2001

Two years ago today Hank was very sick and all the family was at our house. John and Diane brought dinner and went in to see him. John, who had offered to drive Hank's body to Mayfield in a rented van, patted him on the arm and said, "You know Diane and I are going to take you home." Hank nodded yes.

"We're going to wear UK hats and play Merle Haggard music all the way down," John said. Hank whispered a response. I got down close to him and could hear him whisper, "George."

"George?" I asked. He nodded yes.

"George Jones?" John asked and Hank grinned and nodded yes. So it was planned. He was done fighting. He was ready to let go. I am also done fighting and am now ready to let go. He is no longer something I need to cling to. He left me so much, I no longer need to hold on. What is left of him lives inside me.

I spend most of the day with Daddy. He is anemic and they are giving him iron. We discuss Thanksgiving, which is a week away. I am cooking dinner in my new apartment for Cammie, Jacob, India, Roma and Amanda. Daddy said he just isn't up to coming. His hemoglobin is dangerously low. They gave him the option of going to the hospital and having transfusions or taking iron and vitamin C for a week before they test it again. He chose the latter. The nurse said they were going to have a private room with a bath available in the nursing home section soon and they thought he should move there. More change for him. Another holiday season, another crisis looming. Oh, please God, don't let him die through the holidays. We need a calm, normal Christmas! Two years ago Hank had just died and last year James died. We have had enough! I am sick and tired of grief!

It does not seem like the holiday season, but I am prepping for Thanksgiving dinner and looking forward to the kids' visit. We watch videos and play Scrabble and enjoy being together. I treasure this time as I know in years to come they will be too busy to spend much time with me. I remember all the Thanksgivings we went to Tennessee to visit Mother and Daddy and Jennifer when the girls were little. I remember so many past Thanksgivings and Hank is in every memory.

December 2001

I drive by the lot of my new house and can't believe the change. The studs are up separating the rooms. I go home and put up a small tree and set out some candles. The Christmas cactus is blooming again. I feel restless and miss Hank. Life is one big classroom—one lesson after the other and some of the tests are harder than others. I'm thinking about my life with Hank and have to remind myself it wasn't perfect. We were just two normal flawed human beings doing the best we could. I don't want to just remember the good things. I want to remember all of it. I remember Hank preparing for his death. He apologized to me for some things and asked me to write letters to our girls which he dictated to me. Thank God we had the chance to say everything that needed to be said. If I were to die tomorrow, I don't believe I would have regrets or things I need to say. I've done the best I can with my loved ones and friends.

I go to the house and measure windows and walls; the house is now being roofed. I pick out kitchen cabinets and light fixtures. I shop for appliances and will choose flooring next week. It's very exciting and isn't stressful at all. Everything is fresh and new. There are no remnants of death being built into this new house. I collect paint chips and decide to have the kitchen painted bright red. I find an antique fireplace and mantle in an antique shop. It is small and oak and will look so nice in the new house. I like it even more because it came from an old house in Eastern Kentucky.

On this day in 1964 Cammie aspirated a straight pin and it went to the lower lobe of her left lung. We ended up in a hospital in Memphis,

Tennessee where she had lung surgery to remove it. It was an awful time. So near Christmas. There were a couple of days we weren't sure she would survive but she did. Thank God. I remember wondering how I could go back home and face an empty crib if she died. She was 21 months old. Every year on this date I celebrate her life.

Over the holidays, I realize things have shifted. The girls gave me more this year than I gave them and Cammie cooked and fed me for several days. I used to make Christmas happen and this year she did it. I think I'm ready to let her do Thanksgiving too. I went by the house and the front door was installed and locked. I was locked out of my own house. I'll get a key next week.

What will 2002 bring? On New Year's Eve in Mayfield, we always had special food and were with the kids. In Ohio we usually saw in the New Year with neighbors. New Year's in Michigan is kind of a blur. The first few years here in Indiana we were with our group of friends. The last few years we stayed in and celebrated just the two of us. This New Year is a clean slate. No mistakes have been made. Hopefully there will be no family deaths. I'll move into a new home.

I've been thinking about life and how the choices we make lead us down certain paths. I think God has a perfect plan for us, but sometimes we make wrong choices–take the wrong fork in the road–and then the struggle is difficult. I wonder if there is only one special mate for each of us and some people find theirs quickly and others search for years. When I first saw Hank at age 14 I heard a silent voice say, "That's him. I sent him here for you. You will marry him one day." I listened. I knew.

I remember how I felt through the years when Hank was home and I had been away–I would feel so happy when I pulled in the driveway knowing he was there waiting for me. I loved pulling into the house at night, seeing a light on, knowing I wouldn't be alone. I knew I was loved even though Hank had many opportunities through the years to reconsider his choice of me as his wife or to yell at me or call me stupid.

Instead, when those moments came up, he would just grin and hug me. One time, when we lived in Michigan, he pulled over on a busy Detroit highway and taped John Denver and Placido Domingo singing the song "Perhaps Love." He brought it in and played it for me because he said he knew I would love it.

How I have missed that. I don't want to feel something is missing. I want to feel I'm complete. I want to live in the moment and be glad of what I have–not constantly aware of what's missing. I want to accept and embrace my life as it is. If I had died and he had been left, I wonder how he would have done. I'm glad he didn't have to face life without me and grieve like I have done. I wish I could roll back time and Mother and Daddy and Hank and his dad and James could all be alive and healthy again and we could just hit pause long enough to catch our breath.

HANK

(A newspaper clipping Hank asked Jan to retrieve from his files and read to him shortly before his death.)

If I had my life to live over again, I'd try to make more mistakes next time.

I wouldn't try to be so perfect. I would relax more. I'd limber up.

I would be sillier than I've been on this trip.

In fact, I know very few things that I would take so seriously.

I'd be crazier. I'd be less hygienic. I'd take more chances, I'd take more trips,

I'd climb more mountains, I'd swim more rivers, I'd watch more sunsets,

I'd go more places I've never been to. I'd eat more ice cream and fewer beans.

I'd have more actual troubles and fewer imaginary ones.

You see, I was one of those people who lived prophylactically

and sensibly and sanely hour after hour and day after day.

Oh, I've had my moments and if I had it to do over again,

I'd have nothing but beautiful moments-moment by moment by moment.

I've been one of those people who never went anywhere without a thermometer, a hot water bottle, a gargle, a raincoat and a parachute.

If I had it to do all over again, I'd travel lighter next time.

If I had it to do all over again, I'd start barefoot earlier in the spring

and stay that way later in the fall. I'd ride more merry-go-rounds, I'd watch more

sunrises, and I'd play with more children if I had my life to live over again.

But you see, I don't.

-published in the book Living, Loving & Learning, by Leo Buscaglia,

who discovered it in a journal of humanistic psychology

CAMMIE
Memories 1993

I am angry all the time. I don't know what's wrong with me. James and I argue all the time. It wasn't supposed to be this way. Mom and Dad never fought; they weren't angry at each other. I guess that's why I was willing to get married after only knowing James for six weeks. I naively thought that two reasonable adults could work anything out... especially two adults who loved each other and were committed to each other. At least that's how it was when I was growing up. In retrospect, getting married so quickly seems kind of stupid, but at the time it absolutely seemed like the thing to do. And I still don't regret it. I mean, if we hadn't gotten married we wouldn't have India and I wouldn't have Roma and Amanda in my life and we wouldn't have shared the many wonderful moments we have had together. But honestly, I think maybe I'm going crazy. I am angry all the time. And stressed. And we never have enough money.

We are still working out of our house as independent contractors. I am committed to this lifestyle because it allows me to be home with the kids. But we just aren't making enough money. One of us needs to find a job outside the house. The mother in me seems to think that should be James, but apparently the Daddy in him doesn't see it that way because neither of us has yet to find outside employment–in spite of the fact that we are behind on almost every single bill.

So I start fantasizing about my perfect job. I want to make at least $20,000 a year working no more than 20 hours a week. I think that with what James is making as a contractor, that should be enough. I really don't want to work more than that while the kids are little. I'm their mother for goodness' sake–I want to actually mother them. And I really can't imagine getting paid much more than $20,000 a year for part-time work. And though I know there are those who don't think that's very much money, I know others who only make that much working full-time. Either way, it seems reasonable to me. Certainly achievable. As long as I like what I'm doing…I don't want to leave my kids to just go punch a clock and bring in a paycheck. I at least want to be moving in a professional direction.

I think I want to work for a dance organization. I don't really know why. Promoting and managing a dance organization just seems like an interesting use of my journalism and design skills. The fact I know nothing about nonprofit administration is beside the point. I start sitting in the turret every morning, visualizing this fantasy job as I meditate on a limb sprouting out of the fork in the tree outside the window. I see myself sprouting like the limb, venturing out beyond the tree that keeps me rooted. Some time later, I am working 20 or so hours a week at the Fort Wayne Dance Collective, making about $20,000 a year as the Development Director. Go figure. And everyone adjusts. But money is still tight. (Maybe I should have fantasized about more than $20,000 a year!)

"Fort Wayne Dance Collective, this is Allison," I answer the office phone. James is on the line. He is raging mad–I can't even understand what he's saying. I hold the phone away from my ear and wait until he becomes a little more coherent.

Not until I can decipher him saying, "Allison? Allison! Are you there?" do I put the receiver back to my ear. "Yep, I'm here. What's going on?"

"Allison, they turned the water off!" he yells. I was taking a shower and had just gotten all soaped up when the water went off! So I went downstairs wet and soapy and tried to call the water company to see what was going on and the phone wouldn't work!"

Wow. They turned off the water and the phone at the same time– quite a day we're having here. I'm not even surprised–I'm the one who has been shuffling through all our overdue bills.

"So where are you at right now?" I ask him. "What phone are you using?"

"I had to throw on clothes and go over to the neighbors' and use their phone!" he bellows. Okay, I can understand his frustration, but is he just venting or is there a particular reason he's yelling at me?

"You sound pretty angry," I say, trying to affirm and de-escalate. (I have been practicing new communication skills.)

"Allison, are you listening to me?" his voice crescendos. "They turned off our water AND our phone!" he screams in my ear.

Ladies and gentlemen, please put on your seat belts. De-escalation attempts have been aborted; full escalation is ahead.

"And what do you want me to do about it?" I yell back. "I'm AT WORK! If you were at work maybe we'd be paying our bills instead of arguing about our utilities being turned off!" Then again, if we were both at work, who would be home with the kids? Our screaming reduces itself to dead silence. I decide to wait him out.

"Don't you get paid today?" he finally says with strained calm.

"Yes," I say. Thank goodness!

"Then after you get your check, could you please go pay the water bill and the phone bill and get them turned back on?"

"Okay, but you know we're going to have to pay our past due bill and a deposit. If we had the money to do all that we would have paid the bill on-time in the first place!"

"Allison, we can't live without water. And we need a phone. Just do it please!" He hangs up.

Good grief. After I pay all that, there won't be much left of my check. Just enough to get some gas in the car and buy some groceries. Which means the other bills we were going to pay won't get paid...it's an endless cycle and I am weary of it. I am tired of worrying about foreclosure and getting checks to utilities before the date on the disconnect notice. I am tired of living like this.

But there are other moments that are so sweet that I hesitate to make any serious changes. Like Saturday nights on the foutan. On Saturday night, we push the coffee table out of the way, bring the foutan in, turn off all the lights, snuggle up with the kids and watch Are

You Afraid of the Dark? on Nick at Night and eat popcorn. I love the intimacy. I love the simplicity. I even actually love the TV show... I guess I can be cheaply bought because it almost makes everything else worth it. Almost. Of course, everything else is a pretty big catch all. So I just take it day by day.

"Would you please let Hannah out?" I ask 8-year-old Jacob. It is morning and I am scurrying around trying to get breakfast ready before I leave for work. Jacob goes into the back room where the dog sleeps and comes back into the kitchen shrugging his shoulders. "Hannah doesn't want to go out," he says.

I have learned that routine is a magical phenomenon that gives me the illusion that everything is okay–even when I have many reasons to think otherwise. So I cling to routine like it's a security blanket. And our morning routine is that I get up, I get the kids up, we let the dog out, I fix breakfast, we eat, the kids and I get dressed and I go to work. Simple enough. Don't be telling me the dog doesn't want to go out; don't be throwing a cog in this fine-tuned wheel.

I decide to ignore this disruption and move on to the next thing on the list. About the time I am helping India get dressed, I remember the dog still needs to be let out. I am busy with India and Jacob is brushing his teeth so this time I ask James. He goes into the back room and comes back shrugging his shoulders and mimicking Jacob, "Hannah doesn't want to go out."

It is not until I am ready to walk out the door that I finally have a chance to go let her out myself. I march into the back room determined that this time she is going out! The clock is ticking and I am out of time! What is wrong with this dog anyway? I am expecting to see her pacing by the door with a full bladder, but she's not there. Instead I find her lying on her side at the bottom of the stairs...on a pile of newspapers? What is she doing?

I walk over and she looks up at me, but doesn't stand. Oh no, is she sick? I bend down to pet her and ask her what's wrong. She licks my hand and looks a little pathetic. She sighs and shifts her weight. And that's when I see them–six newborn puppies. You have got to be kidding me! No wonder she doesn't want to go out!

She must have made herself a bed with the newspaper and birthed these six puppies in the night by herself, bless her heart. And apparently neither Jacob nor James even noticed! But I am really in no position to point any fingers; I didn't notice she was pregnant.

Well, that's not completely true. In some far-off part of my brain I thought she MIGHT be pregnant, but a pregnant dog was just more than I could deal with. So I conveniently pushed that thought aside; denial is a wondrous thing until reality breaks through. And now reality has arrived. Six sweet, whimpering, fuzzy balls of reality that have yet to even open their eyes. My morning routine is shot to hell; I go looking for Jacob and James.

"Come here, I want to show you something," I say.

"I'll be there in a minute," Jacob says. The proverbial minute.

"I think you're going to want to see this right away." He begrudgingly pulls himself away from his cartoon and follows me into the back room. I take him over to Hannah's nest.

"Do you know why Hannah didn't want to go outside? Look!" I bend down and show him the puppies.

No part of his young brain suspected Hannah might be pregnant– he is truly stunned. And excited beyond measure. He bonds with every single one of those puppies as they spend the next few weeks in our back room.

I don't find this turn of events anywhere near as exciting as he does. Now on top of everything else I am constantly cleaning up after six puppies. If not for Jacob's unabated pleasure, this would be one mess shy of a disaster. Hannah looks exhausted. I empathize completely.

Finally the puppies are old enough to hold their own. James builds them a fence in the back yard and they start spending their days outside. I am counting down to six weeks when we can find them homes.

"You mean we're going to give the puppies away?" Jacob asks after overhearing James and me talking about it.

"Of course we're going to give away the puppies Jacob!" I say without hesitation. "You didn't think we were going to keep six puppies, did you?"

"Well, I didn't think we would keep all six of them," he reassures me, "but I figured we'd keep a couple of them!"

The idea is incomprehensible to me. One dog, two kids, two step-daughters and a struggling marriage in financial disaster is more than enough thank you very much. Add anything else to this full plate and the whole thing is liable to come clattering down. Jacob looks truly stricken.

"Well, maybe we could keep one of them," James chimes in. I cannot believe what I am hearing. No wonder they call him the fun parent!

"I am not keeping any of these puppies!" I proclaim. I wasn't too crazy about getting Hannah in the first place. But a friend who works at the local animal shelter told me they had a dog that would make a perfect family pet and that we should just come look at her and somehow she ended up living in our house...her and her six puppies.

"Well, we don't have to make a decision right now," James says. "We can't give them away for a couple of weeks anyway."

As if that temporary solution solves the problem. All it really does is encourage Jacob to spend more and more time in the back yard. He ends up naming each and every one of those puppies. We have Traveler and Blackie and Patches and Simba and Whitey and Lucky. Each one a beloved ball of energy that Jacob adores.

I cannot believe it when I hear myself finally agree that he can keep one puppy. "Only one!" I warn, trying to salvage some sense of authority. It's as if I am swept up in a wave that just keeps further eroding any sense of foundation.

Jacob ends up choosing Simba because he looks the most like

Hannah. We give all the other puppies away. And shortly thereafter, Hannah runs off. I can't say I blame her, poor thing. But now I sure am glad we kept Simba. James' unique way of seeing the world offers us all so many blessings so much of the time. Why does it all feel so unmanageable to me? I am ashamed to acknowledge that it is almost more chaos than I can bear.

JAN
January 2002

Hank wanted to live to see 2000 so badly and here I am starting 2002. As I enter this new year, I ask myself, What is it I need to be happy and what do I want? I have grown wise enough to know true happiness is not based on external things. True happiness is when I am content and at peace within myself.

Each night I happily crawl into my bed, smile, snuggle between clean, pretty sheets underneath a pretty patchwork quilt, prop up on pillows and read until I am sleepy. Even as a child I loved to go to bed and have always needed a lot of sleep–when I get a good night's sleep I am so thankful.

I go to Florida and go see the Gaither's Homecoming Concert. Hank would have loved that Southern Gospel music. I'm enjoying being with Lita and Ken and the kids and that makes me happy. When I get back to Indiana there will be the last big rush to finish the new house.

While cleaning closets in the Florida suite, I find the box containing cards and notes people sent when Hank was ill and cards he and I gave each other. I cry for a long time. I keep all the ones from family and throw the rest away. I miss Hank, but I do not miss watching the Super Bowl game on TV. He would watch weekend sports on TV for hours and I always hated it.

February 2002

I leave Florida and arrive back in Indiana and go see the house. It is almost finished. I am so pleased.

Tonight I am looking at a black-and-white photograph of my daddy at age 32. I remember this young, healthy man from my childhood. I remember his dark eyes, his handsome, unlined face, his dark, wavy hair. I remember what he and Mother were like together and how I felt safe and loved. I imagine this young man courting the girl of his dreams, marrying her, starting a family and planning a future together. I remember her death and how it changed him. In my mind's eye, I see him today, skinny, shuffling slowly, dependent on a walker or wheelchair, hard of hearing, weak and frail, bowel and bladder problems, confused, wrinkled, white hair, no interests. I am thankful for the daddy he has been to me. I wish I could make things better for him.

I go visit him. He has lost five more pounds and is refusing physical therapy. I point out the therapy might help his legs, so he decides to try. When I start to leave he tries to stand up and falls back down in his chair. I help him up and he hugs me and prays and thanks God for things being as good as they were. He thanks me for helping him with his finances and his room and says he doesn't know what he would do without me.

He hasn't been out of the nursing home since January 1 because he has had an awful cold and is so weak. If the weather is good and he feels like it, I'll take him out soon. I clean out his old room and his attic space and find an old love note Mother wrote him the year before she died. I show it to him and he cries, "Thank Jesus for your mother."

I go visit a week later and he is much worse. He can hardly take even one step. I help him with his coat. "Just like a kid," he says. "I think I will be in a wheelchair full time soon." I agree. He talks about Hank and how proud he would be of me. And how smart Hank was and how much he thought of him.

I go to the house and all the rooms are painted. I love all the colors. Carpet and floors will go down soon, finished surfaces that will hold everything else up.

March 2002

I take Daddy out again and we use a wheelchair for the first time. They are so hard for me to lift in and out of the car. I remember how Hank's wheelchair hurt my back and I would go into back spasms. I am concerned about that now.

The builder and I walk through the house. It is beautiful! We have lunch and sign papers. One of the papers states I am an unmarried woman. I feel shaken. I've thought of myself as married, then wrapped my mind around widowed, but I have never considered myself unmarried. This truth dawns on me slowly. I don't take Hank's picture with me to final closing this time. I'm doing this on my own. But I feel him all around me. He puts his blessing on this house and this move.

I bring three new phones home from the store, struggling to figure out how to work any one of them. I take them back and tell the lady, "I just want an old-fashioned phone that you plug in and when it rings you say, 'hello.' I don't want any fancy stuff or batteries."

Friends help move me from the apartment to the new house. I'm very tired, but can't sleep. This is the last night I will sleep at the apartment. It has been a cozy little retreat, a cocoon. I have felt safe in these walls as I have read, sewed and waited for my new house to be built. It reminds me of when I was 13 and my family rented a large, older, furnished house while ours was being built. That house had a screened sleeping porch where I slept. I loved that summer's ethereal quality, as if we were pretending instead of living our real life. Much like my time here. I have been on hiatus, but it's almost time to begin real life again– a new life in my new home without Hank.

I'm in the new house and it feels good. I take Gloria Gaither's little book "Bless This House" and walk through each room, reading aloud her prayer for that room. I bless my new house. The movers are done by 11 a.m. I work until I can't work any more then take a shower, sit in my recliner and relax. I look at the piles of boxes everywhere and wonder if I will ever restore order. The garage is so full I can't get the car in.

I remember when we moved to Ohio and had a garage for the first time. The houses we lived in Kentucky didn't have garages. We just parked the car in the driveway or on the side of the street. But after we moved, we had a garage that we had to enter at an angle.

One day I pulled in too far over and rammed the car into the side of the garage door. I couldn't move the car forward or back, but in the process of trying I did manage to hit our barbeque grill and tear it up as well. Not knowing what else to do, I finally gave up, got out of the car and left the entire fiasco sitting there.

I dreaded Hank coming home from work and finding the mess I had made. I heard him drive up and waited nervously for him to come inside. After some time had passed without him making an appearance, I mustered up the courage to go out. He was walking around, looking at my handiwork from all sides.

"I can't believe I did something so stupid!" I said. "I wish you would yell at me. I think that would make me feel better!"

"Why should I yell at you?" he asked. "You just made an error in judgment." He started the car and gently rocked it back and forth until he freed it from the side of the garage door. And then we went and bought a new grill.

Surely at some point my new garage will be empty enough that I the car will fit. And when it does, I am confident I can drive it in without mishap! I am happy to celebrate such small victories!

I start unpacking as soon as I got up the next morning. The more I work, the bigger the mess. It seems as if everything I need is under something heavy. I get so overwhelmed I sit in the chair in my bedroom and sob and ask out loud, " How did I ever think I could do this by myself?" I ask God and Hank to help me and get up and start again. Cammie and kids come help. Looking back, I feel terrible that I went to Florida for a few weeks after James died and left Cammie to deal with packing, painting and moving by herself.

I'm very tired. I've worked hard for four hours and then drive over to see Daddy. I feel weary and weepy and nearly fell asleep driving. I take Daddy out to eat. My back is sore from all the moving and lifting and I can't lift the wheelchair, so we use the walker. It has a seat and when he gets too tired to walk, he sits and rests. He has trouble standing and sitting and getting in and out of the car.

"My legs are about gone," he says. He is right.

I cry on the way home, but am not sure what this crying is about. I've been on such a high, vacationing in this little apartment while the house has been built. Now there is hard work and mass chaos and Daddy is getting worse and my back hurts. Hank is really gone. Reality hits. He's not coming home.

My new neighbor comes to visit and we talk a long time. I really like her. She and others offer help. Carl sends a card that says, "Bless this House" and a note that says, "Hank would be proud of you." I cry. God bless this house and bless me as I live whatever days I have left.

HANK

(Excerpts from a work memo Hank authored dated 11/89, found in his desk after his death. He worked as a Quality Control Engineer for a rubber company.)

Most organizations have a planned performance level that they strive to achieve. The daily activities of their people are focused on obtaining that level. However, it seems that forces of nature work against obtaining planned performance levels.

One can think of performance as a ball on an incline plane resting at some planned level. Gravity pulls down on the ball causing it to roll down the plane to a lower level. If we do nothing, performance will get worse simply due to natural forces. To make matters worse, problems occur that put additional pressure on the ball in a downward direction. There is not much we can do about gravity, but we can do something about problems. The catch is, if we only solve problems at the same rate they occur, we will still lose ground. In order to force performance up, problems must be solved at a rate greater than they are occurring.

It is difficult to make progress when we have to spend time and resources solving the same problem(s) over and over. We must discover how to permanently solve a problem so that it goes away forever. Even better would be to find a way to permanently solve similar problems before they ever occur. Prevention is perhaps the most powerful aspect of problem solving. In order to correct a problem AND prevent it and similar problems from occurring in the future, the management system that allowed the problem to occur must be changed. The same old system will allow the same old problems to occur in the future.

Management systems must be fully understood to be effective. Some of them are carry-overs from previous years; these organizational structures may be outdated or obsolete. A careful examination should be made of the management systems and they must be updated when necessary.

CAMMIE
Memories 1995-1998

The sun feels so good on my skin it's almost more than I can stand. I am on the upstairs deck of our Victorian with 5-year-old India. This upper porch has become my favorite part of this big pink house. And the sun feels so good that this moment is quickly becoming my favorite part of this day.

India has her Pocahontas toys spread out on a blanket. I lie down beside her, close my eyes and breathe. A quick body scan makes me mindful of the warmth of the sun on my closed eyelids, my arms, my legs....but I want more.

Spontaneously, I jump up and take off my dress in one swift motion revealing the bathing suit I happen to have on underneath. (It's not unusual these days for me to wear a one-piece under my clothes; somehow it helps me hold myself together.) I lie back down. Oh, so much better! Now I can feel the sun on all those places that were covered up a second ago.

"What are you doing?" India asks. She has stopped playing and is looking at me.

"Mommy's just lying in the sun," I reassure her.

"Why?" she asks.

"Because it feels good."

"But why did you take off your clothes?"

"Because I want to feel the sun all over!"

"Oh, can I lie in the sun too?"

"Sure you can!" I sit up. "We can do whatever we want!" I start scooting toys over to make a place for her to come lie down next to me. By the time I look up, she has ripped off her dress and underwear and is standing there stark naked.

"Oh, that does feel good!" she smiles and prances around. "I like doing whatever we want!"

I am momentarily aghast, but that fleeting feeling is quickly replaced with spontaneous joy. India starts jumping up and down, chanting, "We can do whatever we want!"

I stand up and join her as the creative movement teacher in me takes over. "I can march like this!" I say. We both start marching around the porch as we continue chanting, "We can do whatever we want!"

I quickly realize our chant needs three quarter rests at the end to make it an eight-count rhythmic phrase, so I snort like a pig and jump three times. India squeals with delight, then snorts and jumps with me. One, two, three!

"I can spin like this!" she says and we both start spinning. "We can do whatever we want!" Snort, snort, snort. India squeals again.

My turn. "I can slither like this!" Here we go... "We can do whatever we want!" Snort, snort, snort.

The noise must have called James upstairs because suddenly he sticks his head through the door. "What is going on?" he asks. "India! Put on some clothes!" He looks at me as if to ask, "Have you gone crazy?"

"No!" India protests. "We're playing We Can Do Whatever We Want! And I don't want to put on clothes because the sun feels GOOD, doesn't it Mommy?"

Seeing the look of sheer ecstasy on her face, I smile in agreement. "That's right!" Just for good measure I add a snort, snort, snort. India squeals again and echoes three snorts back. James rolls his eyes and withdraws his head. India and I happily continue our game. Before too long Jacob comes out onto the porch.

"What are you doing?" he asks, surveying the scene. "Why doesn't India have on any clothes?"

"Because we can do whatever we want!" she chants with delight. James must still be upstairs because I hear him say, "Leave them be Jake. It must be a girl thing."

Yes, please, please, just let us be...we dance and chant and snort and snort and chant and dance until we are both exhausted and fall down on the blanket laughing, completely spent. We lay together holding hands, basking in the sun and our joy, our breath heavy from all that exertion. When we can both breathe normally again India asks, "Can we really do whatever we want?"

"Absolutely," I say without hesitation and squeeze her hand. I add no caveats for considering consequences or admonishments about safety or responsibility...I just lay there and enjoy being the fun parent for a change.

Which is something I don't seem to do often enough. I am no longer angry all the time–I am just fed up and disgusted. Our financial situation has not improved. The utilities are all on, but we are behind on the mortgage and as much as I have come to love this house, I am tired of being afraid of losing it. I want out. And James wants to stay. Ever the optimist, he is convinced it will all be okay even though he has yet to propose any sort of plan to substantiate his claim.

It feels like I am living in a time bomb that is liable to explode at any time. And when it goes off, it is likely to rain down an era of homelessness that I would really prefer to avoid. Tick, tick, tick. Apparently, the sound of this bomb is only in my head because he shows no concern. Even so, it has become so loud it has wedged itself into my marriage, creating a dissonance that I can't ignore.

"Allison, where is your wedding ring?" James asks me. We are in the kitchen preparing a meal together. The kids are in the living room watching TV, waiting for dinner. I look down at my left hand. There is the white mark on my ring finger, evidence that a ring has been there, but there is no ring.

"I have no idea!" I am truly stunned and have to stop for a moment and think. Where is my wedding ring? Last I noticed it was on my finger where it was supposed to be. And I don't remember taking it off for any reason. I don't even take it off when I wash dishes or swim...for the past seven years it has lived on my finger. I truly have no idea where my wedding ring is.

"Yeah,' right," James says and turns his back on me, giving his full attention to the vegetables he is chopping. I can't say I blame him. The wedding-ring-must-have-just-popped-off-my-finger story seems pretty unlikely, even to me. Determined to solve this mystery, I start looking for it everywhere. When I brush my teeth, I search the area around the sink. No ring. When I sit down at my computer, I look around my desk. No ring. I look in the car, on the end table by my favorite chair in the living room, around the CDs by the stereo. I look by the fish aquarium, around my meditation spot in the turret and through the toys in the playroom. Where in the hell is my wedding ring? The whole thing is very disconcerting, as if some far-off part of me knows where it is, but won't come clean about it...

It is not until several weeks later that I end up sweeping that ring out from under my bed. There it is in the dustpan! How did it get there? I sit down on the edge of the bed, hold it in my hand and close my eyes, trying to remember. Body memory swells in my right arm. I can feel the weight of that arm as it swings out, then quickly darts towards the floor underneath the bed.

My eyes fly open as understanding washes over me in a cold chill. Oh my gosh! I must have taken my wedding ring off in my sleep and tossed it under the bed! My subconscious dares to speak the truth my conscious mind has been avoiding. I shake my head clear, put the ring quickly back in its rightful place on my left hand, stand up and continue cleaning in a now-desperate attempt to establish some order.

"I see you found your wedding ring," James says later that day. I knew he would notice sooner or later, but I have been dreading the moment. "Where was it?" he asks.

I avoid his eyes. I really don't know what to say, so I decide to go with the truth even though it is certainly far-fetched enough to sound fabricated.

"I found it under the bed while I was cleaning."

"How did it get under the bed?"

"I really don't know. I think maybe I threw it down there while I was sleeping. Bizarre, huh?"

He looks at me. I look at him. I think that is about as much truth as this moment can bear.

But whatever part of me ripped off my wedding ring in my sleep won't be silenced. She is a restless Indian on the warpath. And she is making my life miserable. I tell James I am moving out, but I don't actually leave. Instead, he moves into Roma and Amanda's room. Whether this gesture is an effort to voice his hurt feelings or because he doesn't want to be in close proximity to me, I'm not sure.

But I am still in this house and we are still late on the mortgage and I can still hear the ticking in my head. The whole thing seems such a mess, such a tangled, messed up mess; it is all I can do to get through one day after another.

So I soak in the bathtub and sob. The kids are at my mother's and I'm not really sure where James is right now. I have some blessed time alone and the most I can make of it is to soak and sob. Something needs to change. I feel this urgency to be proactive, but what is the right course of action? I really don't know. I don't even pretend to know. I pray feverishly asking for a sign, for some direction, then get out of the tub, dry off my pruned body and go to bed.

When I wake up, my bedside clock is flashing, telling me that we lost power due to the storm in the night. I'm not surprised. The thunder, lightning and wind was so vicious it woke me up several times. I stumble downstairs for coffee and come back up to the turret for my morning meditation. I look out the window and stop in my tracks. The fork in the tree that has been my focal point for meditation for the past several years has been split apart; it must have been struck by lightning because the entire branch has broken off and is laying in the front yard. And this is no small branch; the base of it has to be at least 3 feet in diameter. James is already out there surveying the damage. I notice that the limb that has been sprouting in the fork, my secret symbol of my emerging self, has been safely left behind and is still green and growing. I can't help but see this as the omen I asked for. But what does it mean? A few days later, my confusion clears.

"Mommy, we made up nursery rhymes today!" India tells me excitedly when I pick her up from school.

"That sounds like fun," I say as I help her into her car seat, making sure she is buckled in before driving off. "Did you make one up?" I ask, pausing for cars as I exit the parking lot.

"I sure did!" she says proudly. "Do you want to hear it?"

"Well of course!" I encourage her.

"Okay, here I go," she says and takes a deep breath as I merge into traffic. "1, 2, 3, 4, kick your husband out the door!"

Oh boy. I feel a little dizzy and grip the steering wheel as I glance at her in the rearview mirror. She is swinging her feet and looking happily enough out the window as she repeats the rhyme in a sing-song voice. I desperately scan my brain for an appropriate response. As appalled as I am, I have to say she did a pretty good job with the assignment: it rhymes, it has meter and it certainly tells a story!

"Good job India," I finally say. As I turn a corner, I realize we both need a little re-direction. "What other rhymes did you hear today?" We sing traditional nursery rhymes all the way home.

As we pull up in the driveway, she says, "My teacher asked if you could come in to the classroom tomorrow morning instead of just dropping me off. She says she wants to talk to you." I bet she does!

India has certainly picked up on the energy in the house, but she only got it half right. I don't want to kick James out; he is welcome to stay. I am moving out. And I am taking the kids with me. I stop thinking about another place to live and start actively looking for one. It needs to be affordable and it needs to be close by and it needs to be a house— I don't want to rip the kids out of this grand Victorian and move them into some small apartment on the other side of town.

It takes several weeks, then a duplex located right around the corner becomes vacant. I go take a look. It has three bedrooms, two bathrooms, a living room, dining room, basement and a fenced in back yard! The master bedroom is large enough for my bed, dresser, desk and computer. And it is affordable. I tell the landlord I'll take it.

He asks for a $350 deposit. I have been putting money aside, a $10 bill here; a $20 bill there. I go home and count my stash. I have $345. I look in my purse and pull out three single dollar bills and make sure I have the rest in change. I take it over to his office and he watches me count it out on his desk down to the very last penny. I think maybe he was expecting me to just write him a check or something because he hesitates. "Are you sure this is what you want to do?" he asks. I flash him a reassuring smile and he sweeps the money up and hands me the lease. As I sign it, my heart pounds an 8-count rhythm: I can do whatever I want, tick, tick, tick!

James helps me pack as we sort through our belongings. You keep this; I'll take that. I'll take this; you keep that. It is a painful process, but we sludge through. I pile boxes and toys and whatnots into the minivan and haul trip after trip around the corner into my new house. This whole process of clearing out starts to feel like some ritualized rite of passage. I make sure and take a piece of the chain-sawed tree trunk that fell in the front yard; it becomes a table for my new back porch.

Finally, we move the big items in the rented truck. In this moment of no return, I no longer feel unsure; instead, I feel...what do I feel? It is almost unrecognizable this feeling, but it is vaguely familiar...it must be...why, it is! It's happiness! And relief! In spite of the fact I am splitting my family apart, I feel happiness and relief.

Friends express sympathy and support when they discover I have moved out. Really, it's okay, I think...the time to have been sorry was during these last several years of indecisive hell. Now, everything finally feels okay.

"If you need anything, let me know," one friend encourages. "I know how overwhelming it can be to have to start doing everything yourself!"

But it seems like the only thing I do now that I didn't do before is take out the trash. I think I can handle it.

Slowly, we settle in. Mother gives me $50 to go buy a foutan. I plop it in the middle of my new living room floor, creating an oasis of calm where the kids and I cuddle every night. And every morning I smile at the Rose of Sharon that is blooming right outside my front door. I finally have a safe place to rejuvenate and prepare for whatever comes next. My heart swells with gratitude as the kids and James and I all adjust to our new life.

James rearranges the things left at the big, pink house to fit this new reality. The kids spend Wednesday and Friday nights with him and go down countless times throughout the week to visit and to play with the dog. Now that we have moved out, James has found a job (!) and Simba spends a lot of time tied up in the back yard. But Simba doesn't seem very happy about it poor thing.

Jacob asks if we can bring him to the new house and I explain that we aren't allowed to have pets here. I don't want to risk violating my lease so I don't even allow him to come visit. Poor Simba. He has no idea where we are; he just knows that we are all suddenly gone and he is left alone, tied up in the back yard.

Until one night I am awakened by the sound of a barking dog. I look at my clock. It is 3 a.m. Whose dog is that and why don't they make it shut up already? The barking goes on and on and on....and it sounds like it is right outside. I finally get up and look out the window. It IS right outside! Simba is standing in our front yard, barking at the house. I go downstairs and open the front door. He quits barking and runs over to me, wriggling all over with happiness.

"What are you doing here?" I ask him. How did he even know where we were? I deliberate my options. I can't just let him stand out here and bark. And I am not walking him down to the big, pink house this early in the morning. For lack of a better idea, I let him into the house. He walks in, goes directly to the foutan and lies down as if he's lived here forever and this is his rightful sleeping place.

Needless to say, the kids are overjoyed to wake up and find him excitedly thumping his tail on the floor in a good morning greeting. I put some water in a bowl and realize I have to talk with the landlord. It appears the dog has moved in.

And thus the separation continues. I have no need or desire to file for a divorce. I am not trying to eradicate James from my life; I just want to establish a sense of security for the kids and me. Since I am no longer contributing to his household expenses, it seem obvious to me that foreclosure looms in our near future. But apparently such things take time because James continues living in the big pink house even though the mortgage is not being paid. (If I had known we could live there for free, maybe I wouldn't have moved out!)

When the furnace goes out, he brings in a space heater and moves into a few rooms on the first floor. It's hard for me to understand why he insists on holding on to this house no matter what, but it's easier for me to allow now that I'm not living in it. By living around the corner, I can watch what happens from a distance. A short distance that allows us access to each other.

Maybe too much access because he is standing in my bedroom in the middle of the night and I am pounding his chest in an enraged fit. I was asleep in my room with all the lights off when I startled awake. It sounded like someone was coming in the front door. I listened again, trying to reassure myself I was imagining things. But no, sure enough, I could hear someone coming up the stairs. (Why isn't the dog barking like crazy?)

Terrified, frozen with fear, I waited through each dreadful step. Unable to muster even an ounce of false bravado or take any courageous action whatsoever, my mind flashed back through the significant moments of my life and quickly rested on my kids. In my mind's eye, I could see them sleeping peacefully in their beds and hoped they would somehow get through this nasty, unexpected turn of events unscathed. I vowed that the intruder would find me so entertaining he would never venture into their rooms. When the assailant finally reached the top of the stairs, the moon that was shining through my bedroom window cast a bigger-than-life shadow on the wall behind him. Not wanting to wake the kids, I didn't scream, but silently willed this looming figure to come through my open bedroom door, away from their rooms. I

t stuck its head in and said, "Allison?" Wait a minute...I fully expected this person coming up the stairs to be some stranger! I can't believe I'm about to be rampaged and killed by someone who knows me! I search the as-of-yet unknown face in the dark.

"James?" I whisper, recognition slowly thawing my brain. I finally find my breath and start screaming. "What in the hell are you doing? You scared me to death!" I no longer care if I wake the kids. Let them know their dad is an idiot! I am up out of bed and pounding him on the chest.

"Allison, stop!" he grabs my arms and disables my attack. I continue my futile wrestling, unable to quiet the energy that is raging through my body.

"What in the hell are you doing?" I ask again. This time I wait for an answer.

"I was going by your house as I was driving home and was concerned because all the lights were off!" he says. "You never turn off all the lights. So I used my key to let myself in and make sure you were okay!"

He knows me well. He knows I hardly ever, almost never sleep with all the lights off. What he doesn't know is that my around-the-corner vantage point allows me to feel safe enough to experiment with new behavior. And not only does he not seem to understand that, he also doesn't seem to understand that in our separated state such things are no longer any of his business.

"Yes, I'm okay!" I say exasperated, finally trying to compose myself. "Or I was until you gave me a heart attack! What is wrong with you?"

That question, unfortunately, goes unanswered. Even as the bank finally reclaims the house and James moves into a downtown apartment. Even as a few years later we write out our divorce agreement and file it with the court. Even as I give our wedding rings back to Mom and Dad.

JAN
March 2002

While going through a box of papers from Hank's study, I run across something I wrote in 1975. Hank was traveling a lot; he would be gone five to seven weeks at a time and I missed him. I wrote about how alone I felt without him and what it would be like if he were to die and be gone forever. Here I am 30 years later, experiencing what I wrote about then.

WHEN I AM ALONE

I am alone when I see the plane take off and part of me goes with it. I am alone when I see the tears running down the faces of all the girls and even though I too am crying inside, I know I must be brave and console them.

I am alone when I go to bed at night and the bed is so big and empty and my feet are cold and there is no one to snuggle close to. I am alone when I hear the alarm ring and go to the kitchen and automatically start the coffee pot even though I don't drink coffee. I am alone when I wake early and work all day and stay up late at night and still can't sleep.

I am alone when I see the Campbell's Soup labels filling up the drawer because you aren't here to take them to the office for a charity; when I get the paper in at night; when the TV sits silently staring at me for hours in the evening; when I see the woodpile and when Jenna sits at the door, wagging her tail waiting for you to come home.

I am alone on Wednesday morning when I gather all the trash

and take it out; when the oven doesn't work and the rope supporting the tree you planted breaks. I am so aware of all that you do for us and how much you care and how often I forget to say, "Thank you." I am alone when you aren't here to see the first snowfall and feel the freezing chill of the cold, cold night.

I am most alone when the end of the week comes. Friday night usually brings a release of tension when we all can lay down the burden of the load we carry and have a pot of chili on the stove and a fire crackling in the fireplace. There is a sense of warmth and love and togetherness and an air of expectancy for what the weekend will hold for us. But this Friday is different. The girls are out with friends, no chili, no fire, no air of expectancy. The house is quiet and still and I am very alone. I have a few moments of realizing this is how it could be when the girls are grown and gone and if you were to die and leave me. It's just a fleeting moment–then I realize how grateful I am for you and our life together and for our girls. I know I would learn to live alone if you were to die and leave me, but I don't know how I would get through it and learn. I'm okay. I read and am relaxed and it's good to know that I have matured and my faith in God is stronger than ever and I can make it even in the deep loneliness of a Friday night.

I am alone on Saturday morning when I wake up and can't go back to sleep. Usually you are at the kitchen table going over our finances on Saturday mornings. It is a good feeling to know you are so capable in this area and that you work hard for us and budget and take care of the bills—but this Saturday the kitchen is empty when I go in there. I am alone when Lita becomes very upset and I reach into the depths of my storehouse of love and wisdom and help her all I can and then she and I pray together and ask Jesus to help her too. I come downstairs and wish you were here so I could talk it over with you. I realize anew how much you share the responsibility of parenthood with me.

I wonder what you are doing today. I know you must be lonely too. I am lonely when the girls and I spend the afternoon at the mall looking at all the things the world has to offer and realize that the only reason we are there is because I don't want to go home to an empty house and spend the long, lonely afternoon without you. We don't spend any money—just minutes and hours. I am more aware than ever of how little all the worldly things would matter if love and companionship were taken our of my world. Now on Sunday night I am not so lonely. I am peaceful and content. Tomorrow starts another busy week full of schedules and work to be done. I will be busy and happy and you will be home Thursday night. Then I can share my experiences and dreams and love with you. Soon we will settle back into the routine of normal living and I will forget the loneliness, but I am thankful for it because it helps me be acutely aware of how much my life, my being, my existence, is wrapped up in you, and I also know that even though many miles separate us, I am really not alone because you are there and you care.

I love you,
Jan

I find the red plaid flannel jacket Hank had on when he died. His jumper. I cry. I've cried more since I've been in the new house than I have in a long time. I seem to be making more messes as I unpack. I get up and look at the mess and chaos in each room and all the boxes still to be unpacked and feel overwhelmed. I start working and get a lot done. It feels so good to flatten each box.

The landscape man comes and we discuss what I want in the yard.

Then it snows 8 ½ inches. I have lots of time to unpack. I keep looking for things I "put in a safe place," like the pearls Hank gave me. I can't seem to find that safe place where I tucked them away.

Jacob and I work in the garage and make room for the car. I take him home and Cammie has a good supper cooked. Her house is clean and orderly and it feels good to be there and rest.

CAMMIE
Dream Spring 2002

The doorbell rings; I open the door and James is standing there. I am stunned. "What are you doing here?" I ask.

"They let me come back!" he says happily, shrugging his shoulders.

I invite him inside. He stands in the foyer of my new house and looks around. James died December 2000; I moved into this house January 2001. It's his first time inside. There's an awkward silence between us.

"Are you tired?" I ask.

"No, I don't really get tired anymore," he says.

"Are you hungry?" I ask. "Can I get you something to eat?"

"No, I don't really get hungry anymore either," he says.

More awkward silence. "How did you get here?" I ask curiously. And then with a sudden rush of excitement, "Hey! Can you drive?"

Maybe he can help me run the kids around to all the places they need to go! He helped with such aspects of parenting when he was alive. Even though our 10-year marriage fell apart, we worked hard at co-parenting. The kids' busy schedule of activities required each of us to take them certain places at certain times. Since his death, I have been trying to maintain that schedule by myself; it is virtually impossible. I simply cannot do by myself what the two of us were able to do together; I physically cannot be two places at one time.

"Can you help me drive the kids around?" I ask excitedly.

"Allison," he says, "I can't drive. I'm dead!"

My anger boils sudden and deep, runs up my spine and explodes out my mouth. "Then what are you doing here?" I yell at him. "And how dare you die! How dare you leave our kids standing at your door in the cold on Christmas Eve! What could you have possibly been thinking?"

"Allison," he says quietly. "Quit yelling at me. I'm dead already. I really don't want to argue with you anymore."

"Well, I really don't want to talk to you anymore!" I say. "I need you to leave." I open the door and he floats out. I close it behind him, go up to bed and go to sleep.

Later, I wake up to something knocking on my bedroom window. I go to the window and see James somehow hovering outside.

"Allison," he says, "you need to let me in. I can't come in unless you invite me."

We look at each other and I think. I think about the kids. I think about the clean palette that this new house provides. I close the blind and turn away.

JAN
April 2002

On Easter, Cammie and kids come for a meal. They are my first dinner guests. They help me with a few things. Jacob and India spend two nights here and India loves being in her own room. She feels more comfortable being in her own room here since this house is on one floor.

Diane and John help put up shelves and hang heavy pictures. We have a good time and laugh a lot. Other friends come in to see the house and bring me gifts and we discuss life changes. Jennifer comes to visit. We spend a lot of time with Daddy. She helps with the wheel chair. She and I talk a lot and share and cry. Neither of us thinks Daddy will live long.

I hurt my back again moving boxes on the porch. I go through boxes of miscellaneous items and find my pearls. I have prayed every day I would find them and am so thankful that I have. I also find a lot of Hank's personal things and cry and cry. I don't want him to be dead. I miss him and would love to share my new home with him. There is danger in being alone so much. It is easy to get used to the quiet of your own routine and get set in your ways. I hope I can always be flexible.

I've been in the house about a month and Jennifer was here a week. Today feels more like a normal day, an absolutely lovely spring day. I have all the windows open and the ceiling fans on. I will put the screened porch in order tomorrow. I can begin to see green in the woods. I put my Bible and devotional books in a large basket by a comfortable chair in my bedroom. I love that this house is all on one floor with no steps to manage.

My cousin calls and my dear, sweet aunt is dying. She and Mother were so close; after Mother died, she was like a mother to me. I'm glad her spirit will soon be soaring. I watch a movie on TV about a college girl caring for her dying mother and cry a lot. I think of Hank's dying.

I think of Mother's dying and wish I'd had a chance to care for her. But I hate thinking my girls may have to care for me.

Today was to have been another normal day, my second in a row. I was going to iron and clean the house. Instead, I get the call that my aunt has died and start packing for the funeral in Kentucky. Death has a way of jerking us from our calm routines into action.

May 2002

Today starts Memorial Day weekend. I feel lonely and restless. I have been so busy for so long, it feels odd to have time on my hands. I am on the screened porch reading. I put my book down and tune in to the symphony of birds. I have a deep sense of inner calm. It is one of those rare moments when I am so aware of my surroundings and blessings. I remember a few similar, fleeting moments: when I was cradling one of my babies; once at Pawley's Island, South Carolina when Hank and I were walking hand in hand on the beach; on our first cruise; once after Hank retired and we were on our back porch.

With the awareness, comes a deep knowing that this moment won't last–it won't always be this way. Life will either change on its own, a series of small and large choices and events that will take me to some place new. Or tragedy may strike, shattering this world into a million pieces in one fell swoop. When tragedy strikes, nothing gets put back together the same way. Tragedy forces us to sort through the shards and find a way to assemble something new, something that can be complete even without the missing pieces.

After tragedy calls, we are never the same person we were before. We either change for the better, become stronger and have a deeper knowledge of our soul and who we are–or we change for the worse, wallow in self-pity and stay crushed and bruised and broken. On this day I sit on my screened porch, listening to the birds, enjoying the woods and my lovely new home, grateful for my health and family and friends and the love I shared with Hank —on this day, I am at peace.

June 2002

I am organizing family photos and feel very lonely. Jessica and Gene are to be married soon and Hank will be absent from those photographs. Years from now when I look back through photo albums, there will be a big black void of Hank's absence. He is already missing from Haley's wedding, Natali's and Sarah's high school graduations, birthdays, college graduations, Jacob starting to drive, the birth of our great nephew and our great-grandbabies and my new home. All of these events are missing Hank's picture. In spite of all the growth I have experienced, my grief remains. It's always there, just below the surface like a shadow. I'm just having a bad night. It will pass. I can choose how I react to my thoughts and feelings. Tomorrow will come and I'll be better.

July 2002

I ride to Mayfield with family and friends to attend my high school class reunion. It is so good to see all these old friends. I thought it would be harder than it is.

August 2002

My life seems to be floating along with no focus or destination. I just live each day as it comes. There is a nice breeze. The birds are singing. The water trickles in the pond. The flowers are beautiful. I relish all the sensations of this lovely morning. In quiet times, I still wonder what life holds for me. For now I'll keep doing what I learned in those first months after he died. I won't let anger or sadness take control. I won't turn into a negative old woman.

HANK

(quotes found in Hank's desk after he died)

We must sail sometimes with the wind, sometimes against it, but we must sail and not drift nor lie at anchor.
    -Oliver Wendell Holmes

Man cannot discover new oceans unless he has the courage to lose sight of the shore.
    -André Gide

We will either find a way or make one.
    -Hannibal Barca, crossing the Alps with war elephants in the 1500s

Keep on going and the chances are you will stumble on something, perhaps when you are least expecting it. I have never heard of anyone stumbling on something sitting down.
    -Charles Kettering

Behold the turtle; he makes progress only when he sticks his neck out.
    -James Bryant Conant

Act as if it were impossible to fail.
    -Dorothea Brande

Our chief want in life is somebody who will make us do what we can.
    -Ralph Waldo Emerson

CAMMIE
Dream Fall 2002

I am walking up a mountain on a wooded path. As I near the top, I come across a man sitting by a cave cooking food on a fire. He asks if I'm hungry and invites me to share his meal with him. I sit down beside the fire and wait for him to finish preparing it. He happily chatters and whistles as he works. After watching for a while, I realize he has positioned himself so that everything is within reach; I have yet to see him move away from the spot where he is sitting. We enjoy a lovely dinner. While cleaning up, I realize he doesn't have use of his legs; I watch him walk on his hands and drag his lower body behind him. Though this slows him down somewhat, he doesn't seem to mind.

"What happened to your legs?" I ask.

"Oh, they don't work anymore," he says nonchalantly, without explanation. I suppose a look of horror flashes across my face because he quickly adds, "It's okay. I don't really need them anyway. It's amazing what we can really do without."

I have nothing to say so he continues, gesturing to the cave. "I live in this cave now and am quite happy, " he says. "Actually, it's amazing how comfortable I am. I really didn't need all that stuff we had when I lived with you and your mother and your sisters. "

Huh? When he lived with us? I look at him more closely and see a slight resemblance hidden underneath the shag and scruff.

"Daddy?" I ask hesitantly.

"You finally recognize me!" he beams. "I was wondering how long it was going to take you to realize who I was. I knew who you were right away!"

"What happened to you?" I ask. "What are you doing here?"

He looks around and shrugs his shoulders. "I'm not sure," he says dismissively. "This is just where I ended up." I help him as he continues cleaning up after the meal. I am disturbed by how primitive everything is. We are sitting in dirt. His bed is a pile of leaves. He is wearing animal skins and using self-made tools. How can he possibly be happy here?

"Daddy," I say. "Come home with me. I'll take you home."

"Oh no," he says emphatically. "I'm not going anywhere."

"But why?" I ask. "Look at this place. You're living in filth and poverty and you can't even walk...Daddy, you don't have to live this way. There are people who love you and miss you! There are people who can help you. Please, come home with me!"

"But I don't need any help," he says. "Come look!" He drags himself to the nearby mountain edge. "Once I reached the top, there was only one place left to go..."

I scream and lunge for him as he launches himself over the edge. I rush to lean over and look, expecting to see him careening into the abyss. Instead he swoops up and out, flying over the landscape of valleys and rivers and trees. I watch his aerial dance of joy and stand speechless as he lands at my feet, once again supporting himself with his hands, dragging his useless legs behind him.

"Just because I can't walk doesn't mean I can't fly," he jokes. "And flying is actually a lot more fun!"

"Don't worry about me," he continues, more seriously. "I always said if it wasn't for your mother and you girls, I'd be happy living in a cave. So, here I am. Now go live your life and climb your own mountain. And when you get to the top, don't stand safely at the edge; make sure you give yourself the opportunity to jump off and fly!"

I hug him goodbye, walk back down the mountain and go home.

JAN
September 2002

I have Hank on my mind all day. All night I dream about him and mesothelioma and sickness and death. I wake knowing it is my 62nd birthday and I feel happy. I celebrate with friends and family over several days. Hank's life was cut so short, maybe I'm trying to live life for him too.

October 2002

Jessica and Gene are married. At the wedding, they show a video that includes Hank holding Jessica when she was a baby and another of him with her dressed up to go to a dance. Jessie and Gene are just starting out on their journey of marriage and life; I think back to our wedding day and how happy and in love we were.

November 2002

It is the third anniversary of Hank's death. I remember at first thinking I couldn't survive the pain of his absence, but I have. Sometimes it still hits me suddenly, from out of nowhere. But I strive to live my life with dignity and humor and joy and thankfulness. I am blessed with normal, routine days. The leaves are beautiful–gold and orange with a little red. I am happy and content and grateful. I have joy in my soul. My world is a good place to be.

Dear Hank,

Three years ago tonight your spirit flew and I believe you are in the presence of God, hanging around the eastern gate waiting for me. What a journey it has been for me since that night your physical presence left me. I remember a few weeks before you died the nurse was visiting and asked how we kept such a positive attitude with our world shrinking as it was. I told her if we could just keep things as they were we would be content. It didn't matter we couldn't go out and lead a normal life–we would be content if we could just sit in our recliners and let our feet touch. (We called it 'foot sex').

But the pain came, the cancer spread, your quality of life was gone and we had to accept that it was time to release you and let you go. You were so brave to teach me so many things that would help me when you were gone and to tell me so often that you loved me and to leave me the letter to be opened after your death. Oh, how I loved you! Our love was so deep in the beginning, then mellowed and strengthened and became more intense as the years passed and we fell in love all over again. We took that love to a different level during your illness. I hope you knew how much I loved you and appreciated what you did for our family—all the sacrifices you made. I told you often enough.

It was so good to hear you come in the door after work and so good to be together all the time after you retired. I remember us playing dominoes on the screened porch and enjoying our backyard woods. I remember us turning off the lights and dancing in the family room to soft music and candlelight. I remember that all-is-right-in-the-world feeling when we would be in the same room together—you watching sports on TV and me doing needlework. I remember those first weeks and months after you died; the pain and grief was so acute it was almost more than I could bear at times, but the writing I began the night you died and reading the books on grief really helped me and I have healed.

Here I am three years down the road on my journey to find myself without you and I am happy and content and anticipating what life has for me. I no longer have clenched fists, but open hands ready to receive the blessings that will come my way. I'm so thankful to have shared your love and your life. Thankful I have grown and flourished rather than withered and dried up. I've grown used to being alone and doing what I want when I want. I guess you can find good in any situation if you just look for it.

Today was warm and sunny with colored leaves everywhere. A perfect fall day, just the kind you would have loved. If you were alive and well, you would have walked in the woods, raked leaves, cut firewood. I can close my eyes and see you in your red plaid jumper and non-jogging suit.

So my dear Hank, until I am with you again–I'm doing well. I hold you in my heart and will always remember. As your tombstone says, "May the Lord watch between you and me when we are absent one from the other." Genesis 31: 49

Love,
Jan

EPILOGUE

JAN
January 2010

It's been ten years since Hank died. Ten years. When I read the pages of this book, I experience most of the same emotions I felt when it was all actually happening. I laugh and I cry. I've learned that I haven't gotten over the loss of Hank; I've just become used to it and have learned to weave his loss into the fabric of my present life.

I'm at a good place. I'm almost 70 years old and have a calm, quiet life. I'm still enjoying living in the new house. I am in good health and have good friends. I feel blessed that all my family is also in good health and I get excited every time a grandchild gets married or there is a new baby in our family. I have learned that entering and departing our world is hard work; the labor of birth and dying are both lonely jobs.

My daddy, Wayne Holman, died February 2003. He was so weak his neck couldn't support his head; I sat on the floor and looked up at him so we could make eye contact. He told me he was ready to die. He said he was tired and had no joy in living and he started refusing food, water and medicine. He died 10 days later. He doesn't need a wheelchair anymore.

I still miss my old life when Hank and I were a party of two, but I am content with my new life. I've learned that the number one can be a complete number. I like the person I have become. I'm so glad I worked hard at dealing with all aspects of my grief so I could become this new woman. I think Hank would be proud of me. If Hank could come back to Indiana and visit for a few minutes, I think he would hold me close and say:

Jan, I am so proud of you. I knew this would be the hardest thing you have ever done but I also knew you could do it–I knew that you were stronger than you thought. I'm glad you not only survived my death, but are thriving.

I like the new house and am glad you don't have steps to climb and I love the woods and the screened porch. It reminds me of the house in the woods that we shared together. You did a good job decorating it. I really like the red kitchen.

I look at all the family pictures you have and I am amazed at how the kids have grown. It's so nice to see pictures of all the new family members—those acquired through marriage and also all these new babies! It's hard for me to believe you are a great grandmother—and it's hard to believe Babs and Lita have grand-children and that baby India is in college. And I never imagined Jacob would be so tall…

And so our family story continues without Hank's physical presence, but with the memories we have of our time with him. I'm glad he was in my life and I'm glad I've found peace and contentment without him.

EPILOGUE

CAMMIE
December 2009

I can't seem to get warm. The cold seems to follow me around the house even though the thermostat says I shouldn't be feeling this way. I go to my closet to get something to put on and the worn, grey sweater I stole from Daddy when I was a kid falls off the hanger. I haven't worn this sweater in years. I smile and put it on and feel better.

Later I go to the coat closet to get out the vacuum cleaner and come face to face with an alpaca sweater Daddy brought me from one of his trips to South America. I haven't even seen this sweater in years...in spite of the fact that I have been looking for it. How could I have missed it if it was hanging right here? Merry Christmas to me! I put it on too and finally begin to warm up.

But I can't seem to shake this unsettled feeling. It lingers like a fly that just won't go away. I keep glimpsing something in my periphery, but when I turn to get a full view, there's nothing there. I am washing dishes when I feel it truly sneak up behind me, full force. I freeze suddenly, my hands still in the soapy water, completely aware that I am in the presence of... something...what? I am not afraid. I am waiting. I am listening.

"Finish the damn book!"

The voice is loud and clear. And male. And exasperated. An exasperated voice of authority that sounds strikingly like the voice that once told me to get my ass on a plane!

"Daddy?" I venture cautiously. And laugh. Of course it's Daddy!

"How are you doing?" I ask him casually as I continue scrubbing the dish in my hand.

"Finish the damn book!" he says again. Still not one for too many words, is he?

I make sure and set aside time over Christmas vacation to re-read this manuscript that has evolved slowly over the past 10 years since Daddy and James both died. I am glad I have time to curl up with it, to absorb it. I cringe from the intensity of all this pain and the depth of all this sorrow...and I am grateful for the strength, courage and clarity that surfaced in the midst of all this adversity.

"Did all this really happen?" I ask Mother and myself. "Surely we must have made this up...at least some of it."

"We most certainly did not make this up!" Mother says emphatically without hesitation. "It most certainly did happen! Every bit of it!"

And so it did. This is our story. Part of it anyway. A big part with many subtexts that continue to shape who we are as individuals and as a family.

In May 2009 Jacob graduated from college and now works as an industrial designer, a job for which he has great passion. India graduated high school with honors and is now in college discovering what she wants to do and be. Roma is a pharmacist and Amanda a geophysicist and all our relationships are intact and have continued to grow and deepen in love and understanding. Over time, I have watched all my kids process their own grief in their own way (or not), establish their own intimate relationships (or not), identify and pursue their own goals and mature as good people living lives balanced by focus and fun. More or less. Or so it seems...

To tell the truth, I think few of us fully understand or grasp what's really going on around us most of the time. But a few things I know for certain:

- Much of what we think of as "reality" is nothing more than illusion with any number of parallel "truths" that are constantly taking new forms;
- The only true constant is change; the key is learning to direct it through deliberate co-creation; and
- One must claim root happiness with steadfast vigilance – surface

emotions may fluctuate with daily events, but root happiness is not situational; it must be core.

I am proud and relieved to be able to say I am happy. Busy, challenged and happy. James and I have posthumously forgiven each other for whatever we did or didn't do that we should or shouldn't have...I realize we did the best we could and I am grateful for our memories and our love. I am proud of my kids. I have a comfortable lifestyle. I like my work and am supported and appreciated by a community network that I respect and that I think respects me. I am strong and healthy and have established meaningful relationships with people I care about. My mother is still alive (thank goodness!) and we still live near each other and talk regularly. And I feel connected to a deep spiritual purpose: to love, learn, create, inspire and serve in joy. Enjoy.

I am proud and relieved to say I did complete graduate school and was awarded a Master of Arts in Dance/Movement Therapy from Columbia College Chicago in January 2003. It took me four years to complete this two-year program that required 60 hours of coursework, 1,500 hours of fieldwork and a thesis. It was a big bite to chew in the midst of the death storm that hit; it almost swallowed me whole. But I bit back, sunk my teeth in deep and shook it for all it was worth. And I'm glad–I'm glad I did it and I'm glad it's done!

And it serves me well. I am still self-employed and work as an independent contractor writing grant proposals for non-profits (and now apparently life stories!). I am also the founder/Director of Fort Wayne Taiko and work as an artist in residence teaching movement and rhythm programs to various groups at schools, community organizations and conferences. And I write, create, and direct multi-media performance art working with children, youth, adults and special need groups.

Basically, I play. A lot.

On this cold winter night, on the eve of another new year, I am grateful to say I claim my happiness with steadfast vigilance. I stake a claim for this present moment, for my future and for the future of my family...and for our history. I write this to my Dad. And to James. And my children. I sing it to the stars and whisper it to the moon as I dance under a sky framed by bare December trees. I drum as the vibration of life's windy rhythm blows through me in waves...I stand strong, a figure-head facing the full force of the gale head on.

So it is. So may it be.

WHAT CANCER CANNOT DO

Cancer is so limited...
It cannot cripple love.
It cannot shatter hope.
It cannot corrode faith.
It cannot eat away peace.
It cannot kill friendship.
It cannot shut out memories.
It cannot silence courage.
It cannot invade the soul.
It cannot reduce eternal life.
It cannot quench the spirit.
It cannot lessen the power of the resurrection.

-Anonymous

234699LV00003B/1/P

9 781432 773816